My Japanese trainers at Toyota could masterfully take a complex subject and explain it and teach it so wonderfully simple. It didn't make it any easier, but it made it possible for me to now do. Ledbetter has done just that with *The Toyota Template*. He lays out the entire, and complex, Toyota Production System (TPS) in a basic and understandable manner that will make it possible for you to do also. His perspective and focus on "Just in Time" material availability and "Flow-Pull and Leveling" are missing components in many failed lean attempts. And his connection and integration to the "Respect for People" culture side of the Toyota Way makes this a "must read" for any "continuous learner" of Lean.

Mike Hoseus
Former Toyota Executive and Co-author of Shingo Award Winning book, Toyota Culture.

Through his personal experiences, Phil clearly and succinctly explains how to implement a Lean strategy based on TPS principles and practices. It is essential for every company embarking on their Lean journey to understand that Lean is based on *The Toyota Template* and is not just a collection of tools. This is a must-read book for all lean practitioners and executives of Lean companies.

Nick Katko
BMA, Inc., Author The Lean CFO.

Drawing on his extensive experience, Phil Ledbetter shares his insights into the foundational principles of the Toyota Production System. This book will give you a deeper understanding of what has made Toyota successful and a practical application that you can use to develop your own transformation.

Jim Garrick
manager, Global Operational Excellence & Process Improvement, Southeast Regional Director – AME, Shingo Prize Examiner.

In The *Toyota Template*, Phil Ledbetter details his first-hand experiences and shares the knowledge of the creators of the Toyota Production System. From these, he forges a template that will work in any enterprise, any system, any process. *The Toyota Template* is Just-In-Time for the company starting, struggling, or seeking to achieve the results of the vaunted Toyota Production System.

Michael Lewis
Director of Operations, ThyssenKrupp Elevator;
TMMK Team Member 1989–2001.

The Toyota Template
The Plan for Just-in-Time and Culture Change Beyond Lean Tools

By

Phil Ledbetter

CRC Press
Taylor & Francis Group
Boca Raton London New York

CRC Press is an imprint of the
Taylor & Francis Group, an **informa** business

A PRODUCTIVITY PRESS BOOK

CRC Press
Taylor & Francis Group
6000 Broken Sound Parkway NW, Suite 300
Boca Raton, FL 33487-2742

© 2018 by Phil Ledbetter

CRC Press is an imprint of Taylor & Francis Group, an Informa business

No claim to original U.S. Government works

Printed on acid-free paper

International Standard Book Number-13: 978-1-138-57871-5 (Hardback)

Library of Congress Cataloging-in-Publication Data

Names: Ledbetter, Phil, author.
Title: The Toyota template : the plan for just-in-time and culture change
beyond lean tools / Phil Ledbetter.
Description: Boca Raton : Taylor & Francis, 2018. | Includes index.
Identifiers: LCCN 2017040742 | ISBN 9781138578715 (hardback : alk. paper)
Subjects: LCSH: Just-in-time systems. | Production control. | Corporate
culture. | Toyota Jidōsha Kōgyō Kabushiki Kaisha.
Classification: LCC TS157.4 .L434 2018 | DDC 658.5--dc23
LC record available at https://lccn.loc.gov/2017040742

Visit the Taylor & Francis Web site at
http://www.taylorandfrancis.com

and the CRC Press Web site at
http://www.crcpress.com

My book is dedicated to my mama, Louise. In appreciation

for the witness her life has been for her children Phillip,

Sherrie, and Melanie. Love you, mama!

Contents

Preface xi
Author xiii

Chapter 1 The Problem: Distance from Toyota 1

    Endnote 3

Chapter 2 The Predicament: Perplexing Failure 5

    Endnotes 11

Chapter 3 The Position: Plant First 13

    Endnotes 14

Chapter 4 The Purpose: Will and Skill 15

    Endnotes 19

Chapter 5 The Plan: Hoshin Kanri 21

    KPI Rules 23
        Measuring Overall Progress 24

Chapter 6 The Property: Waste Elimination 27

    OHNO'S 7 Wastes 28
        Overproduction 28
        Waiting 29
        Transportation 29
        Over-Processing 30
        Excessive Inventory 30
        Unnecessary Motion 31
        Defects 31
    5S 31
    Endnotes 34

Chapter 7 The Practice: Standard Work 35

    Total Productive Maintenance (TPM) and Machine
Back-Up: Tension in the Line 37
Teamwork: The Multi-Skilled Employee 39
Endnotes 42

Chapter 8 The Patois: 8-Step Problem-Solving 45

    Endnotes 56

Chapter 9 The Pattern: Flow, Pull, and Heijunka 57

    Continuous Flow: Alignment of Processes in the Order
of Value Added 58
Pull: Paces and Prioritizes Production, and Promotes
Problem-Solving 60
Kanban: Metering Flow 67
Heijunka: Production Smoothing 68
Single-Minute Exchange of Dies (SMED): Set-Up Time
Reduction 72
Endnotes 75

Chapter 10 The Program: Jidoka, Quality at the Source 77

    Endnotes 79

Chapter 11 The Path: The Toyota Template 81

    When Should the Template Be Implemented? 82
In What Order Should the Template Be Implemented? ... 82
Endnotes 86

Chapter 12 The Proof: TPS Results 87

    Environment 89
Endnotes 92

Chapter 13 The Perceptions: Mental Images 93

    Endnotes 94

Chapter 14 The Post Script: Personal Matters......................................95

Index..97

Preface

Much has been written about Toyota over the last 30 years. Not only because they make great cars but also due to interest in the Toyota Production System. The Toyota Template is no different in that regard. It's about the critical concepts and methods that Taiichi Ohno implemented in developing the Toyota Production System. Where it is different is in the parallels it draws between Toyota's pre-Toyota Production System condition and companies today that are attempting to become more efficient or "lean."

In view of efficiency, or "leanness," many organizations are in the same position as Toyota was prior to implementing what was once called the "Ohno System." This system was developed over many years through problem-solving and trial and error. The building of the Toyota Production System, with the goal of eliminating waste, evolved as problems were encountered and solutions put in place. A wonderful byproduct of these years of work was the growth of a problem-solving culture throughout Toyota that is unique in the business world.

Today, the Toyota Production System is well established. Though it is constantly improving, the historical picture is visible. The question many have tried to answer for their own companies is "How can they achieve world-class efficiency?" The Toyota Template answers this question. It explains the critically important elements of the Toyota Production System, analyzes the sequence of implementation as the system developed, and puts these elements in a logical order of implementation based on history and current knowledge. Additionally, it addresses the effect of each element on the culture.

There are really two reasons for writing this book. The first is due to my personal observations of the failure of most attempts to develop lean systems. Much of this is because the reason for the success of the Toyota Production System has been ignored. It's been said:

> Many good companies have respect for individuals, and practice kaizen and other TPS tools ... But what is important is having all the elements together as a system. It must be practiced every day in a very consistent manner, not in spurts.[1]

The elements have not been put "together as a system" and "practiced every day in a very consistent manner." Most attempts have been focused on bits and pieces of the elements, or the tools.

The second reason is more personal. I have become concerned that because successful lean implementations are so rare, this reflects poorly on the Toyota Production System. Having worked in management at Toyota for 15 years, I feel a certain responsibility to prove that their production system is, as Ohno said, "a concept in management that will work for any type of business."[2]

The resources I used to write this book came from my personal experience of learning about, and managing in, the Toyota Production System at Toyota Motor Manufacturing Kentucky in Georgetown, Kentucky. Every day was a learning experience. I've often said that my experience at Toyota was more valuable to me than my college degree. In addition to my own experience, I leaned primarily on the writings of Mr. Ohno and a handful of others who were present during the development of the Toyota Production System. In fact, the book is sprinkled with quotes from Mr. Ohno in support of directional validity of the Toyota Template.

Finally, as you read this book, do so with your own business in mind. Try to imagine how the Toyota Template could be implemented at your workplace to achieve efficiency and a problem-solving culture.

With passion,

Phil Ledbetter

ENDNOTES

1. Liker, Jeffrey K. 2004. The Toyota Way, *14 Management Principles from the World's Greatest Manufacturer*, p. 27. New York, NY: McGraw Hill.
2. Ohno, Taiichi. 1988. *Toyota Production System: Beyond Large-Scale Production*, p. 9. New York, NY: Productivity Press.

Author

 **Phil Ledbetter** is a passionate advocate of the Toyota Production System and the many benefits it can provide for business. He worked as a leader in management with Toyota Motor Manufacturing Kentucky for 16 years. As group leader, he learned, practiced, and taught the many elements of the Toyota Production System. He was certified as a kaizen leader, enabling him to teach other members of the management team problem-solving. In his time at Toyota, he was immersed in all aspects of Toyota Production System.

Phil is an accomplished teacher and conference speaker, having developed classes for and taught hundreds of employees on all aspects of the Toyota Production System. Since leaving Toyota, Phil has been instrumental in the implementation of various Toyota methods in several different industries.

Phil is a graduate of the University of Kentucky. He's the father of a son and daughter, and the proud "Poppy" of five grandchildren. He resides in the Nashville, Tennessee area.

1

The Problem: Distance from Toyota

Problems require solutions.

The lean world has become an interesting place over the years. Lots of companies in many different industries all over the world have been, and are, attempting to implement lean systems. However, the overwhelming rate of failure is hard to understand. Most estimates are in the 90% range, some even higher. I've often wondered why this is so. What's the problem? As I considered my experience at Toyota, researched the history, and observed what's been going on, many thoughts came to my mind.

It's well known that Toyota has been the gold standard for any company attempting its own lean implementation. People from all over the world have toured the Toyota plant in Georgetown, Kentucky, over many years. Even though I worked there, I've taken the public tour myself a few times out of curiosity. What people see on the tour is the current product of the Toyota Production System (TPS), which took many years, through trial and error, to develop.

> [T]he Toyota Production System evolved gradually, step-by-step. Taiichi Ohno, Kikuo Suzumura, and others conceived elements of the system and worked heroically to put their concepts into practice. But none of those individuals ever possessed a comprehensive vision of the Toyota Production System as an integrated framework. They were simply tackling problems that arose in the workplace, one by one, and their solutions accumulated and gradually became—collectively—what we now know as the Toyota Production System.[1]

Toyota has been very open with their system since arriving in the United States. The extreme example was their 25-year joint venture from 1984 to 2009 in Fremont, California with General Motors (GM), called NUMMI.

GM had full access to every part of the production system and training from hundreds of Toyota trainers. Yet, it has proved very difficult for them and others to implement real lean systems that approach the efficiency of Toyota. As I pondered this reality, my mind repeatedly arrived at the obvious question. Why?

Many companies that are successful, or at least making money, have decided, albeit cautiously, to take the plunge to become efficient. These companies have employed many resources, including outside help and benchmarking visits to those places they believe to be helpful, and spent a lot of money on production boards, kanbans, returnable dunnage, and any number of tools in search of a lean culture change, reduced costs, and world-class on-time-delivery.

These are good companies, with good products that are in demand in the market, that are looking for improvement that differentiates them from their competitors. Either they realize that there's room for improvement or they fear falling behind the competition. Either way, from an efficiency standpoint, companies today are in a similar position to that of Toyota prior to the development of the TPS. They're running with the herd. And, let's be honest, there's some safety in the herd. Excessive inventory, unsynchronized production, poor housekeeping, and excessive costs are common problems today, just as they were at Toyota many years ago. Unfortunately, many don't realize they have problems, because they're comfortably settled in with the herd.

Since companies today are in a similar starting position, wouldn't it make sense to understand what Toyota did when they were in this same spot? If we agree that Toyota is the leader and best example of a "lean" company, wouldn't it be instructive to examine the Toyota record to understand what they did, why they did it, how they did it, and the results? And how did the steps they took lead to the development of that elusive lean culture?

Once the what, the when, the why, and the how are deeply understood, wouldn't there exist a template for a successful lean implementation? Absolutely! If companies today that strongly desire to become efficient manufacturers, world class in their markets, were to set about following this "Toyota Template," shouldn't it follow that they could become efficient and world class? Yes!

The fact is that a successful and sustainable lean production system and culture requires the implementation of the "Toyota Template." In fact, it's the only way to become an efficient, just-in-time company. TPS is the benchmark for all lean initiatives. In this book, I'll examine the key steps and concepts Toyota took under the leadership of Taiichi Ohno, with the full support of Kiichiro and Eiji Toyota, and develop this Toyota Template.

The Problem: Distance from the Toyota Template. Lean efforts are far away from the TPS.

Culture: Culture is not grown through tools. The culture developed because of the steps Ohno took over time.

ENDNOTE

1. Shimokawa, Koichi and Fujimoto, Takahiro. 2009. *The Birth of Lean*, p. 129. Cambridge, MA: The Lean Enterprise Institute.

2

The Predicament: Perplexing Failure

Predicaments are where we find ourselves when we take actions or make plans based on our beliefs, but it turns out we're wrong.

Each idea was conceived and developed in response to a need.[1]

Several years ago, I was asked, "What's your favorite lean tool?" I was surprised and taken aback by the question. As I pondered my response, it occurred to me that I had never thought about the Toyota Production System (TPS) in that way. I never had a favorite tool. Tools weren't addressed in this way at Toyota. We didn't discuss our favorite tools at lunch. What's going on here? Initially, I wasn't sure if this was a serious question or not. But as I looked around the room, I realized that these people were truly interested in my favorite. I could not disappoint them! Hesitatingly, my response was, "Whichever tool is appropriate for the problem." The reaction was a blank stare. How could I be a "lean guy" and not have a favorite lean tool? I wondered if they thought I was skirting the question. Later, I realized that the questioner, and everyone else, had a very different viewpoint. In fact, everyone in the room shared this view. TPS was not a management system, as I'd experienced. It was a collection of interesting tools, one of which should be my favorite. Kind of like my favorite ice cream flavor, I suppose? In the years since, I've come to realize that this is not an uncommon view of TPS.

The majority of "lean transformations" are, and have been, tool oriented. This is the most common understanding of what lean means, even to many who say otherwise. In terms of culture change, many leaders talk about it, but usually in a mythic way. It's as if talking about behavioral models and learning methods will make culture change a reality. It seems as if education on lean concepts is the key to changing the way people think. Putting a few tools in place will, somehow, change the culture. People just need to have the concepts explained to them, participate in a few "kaizen events," use the terms, and "POOF!" we're on our way to efficiency. This is tragic for business. In so many situations, a tool is rolled out as the solution to some problem. If parts are put on kanban or a 3P is done in an area or an hour-by-hour board is put up at some line, then we have the solution, right? I've even witnessed several countermeasures over the years that are nothing more than data collection methods. It's crazy! Of course, I have no problem with any of the Toyota tools. They were developed and/or adopted as countermeasures to problems Toyota encountered while developing their production system. But is this tool approach the way to a lean enterprise? Based on history, I think not.

A good example of this tool emphasis is the Value Stream Map (VSM). This tool has become the first must-do in many lean efforts, almost as if it were an antidote for the problem. If this were the first step to becoming efficient, why didn't anyone who was involved in the development of TPS ever mention it? Looking back, I would think that this tool would have been a major part of my education at Toyota. Seems like we would have talked about it regularly? It's hard to believe that Toyota would hold such a seemingly critical tool back from us.

Alas, given its widespread popularity, what is interesting about the VSM is that it was not developed at Toyota. Apparently, it was based on a comparatively lightly used tool called a Material and Information Flow Diagram (MIFD).[2] The MIFD was generally used with suppliers to understand the direction of material and information flow through their processes. This is understandable, as the MIFD would quickly show whether a supplier was using a pull system or a push system. This would be important to know. A well-known blogger's research gives several examples of the MIFD, used in publications about Toyota and Nissan, but he observes that "Their purpose is to explain, not to document a current state or design ideal and future states. They don't use a standard graphic language, and are not bound by the strictures of VSM."[3]

The VSM is a snapshot in time of the current condition as it pertains to inventory/work in process (WIP), cycle times, total lead times, number of operators, value-added time, changeover times, batch sizes, and any other measures you decide to include. Keep in mind that this is a snapshot. It also shows the information flow through the processes from start to finish. After making a current state map, the idea is to follow up with a future state map. The future state map should represent the desired future condition. This is all interesting information. But is it useful?

One problem is that the VSM tends to point to symptoms. The detailed information about WIP between processes, lead times, and cycle times leads to a focus on these particular findings. The tendency is to concentrate efforts on these pieces of the puzzle as opposed to the system as a whole. Remember that what makes Toyota special is "having all the elements together as a system."[4] Elements? What elements was he talking about?

In manufacturing, there are two basic operating systems. The first, and most common, is a push system. In this scenario, the various operations on the floor use schedules for production. The schedules are based on projected demand over a period of time, say a week. They are then delivered to each process where production is to begin. Generally, if each area has one schedule per day, the processes will either make their products in some predetermined order or make them in the order that best maximizes their process. Keeping in mind that each order on each schedule must mate up with other orders on the other schedules, a problem surfaces. That problem is timing. These various processes don't run at the same pace, and many times the orders are not run in a cohesive sequence. These timing issues show up in the lack of synchronization between orders that must mate up to be completed or sold.

To deliver the finished product to the customer and collect the money, these various individual orders must come together during production or in shipping. If they don't sync up during production, the result is waste. This can be in the form of wait time at the locations where the orders need to mate up, or it could result in overproduction of orders while waiting, or both. Also, some orders may arrive in shipping days ahead of their mates or days behind, resulting in products that cannot be delivered until their mates arrive.

> Looking at things individually they say they are doing a good job of producing gears, or that they are using robots very well, or that they can do the work with just 3 people. But these items can only be sold when they are together as a set.[5]

Push systems do not synchronize, nor do they pace production through the plant. Instead, each individual line or process runs to its own pace on its own schedule. Some orders go to batch build processes, while others start on one-piece flow lines. These timing issues affect synchronization. And in a push system, it's difficult to tell the normal from the abnormal. Which area is behind, which orders are too early? There are many problems associated with push systems.

When operating in a push system, as most companies do, it should come as no surprise to see minuscule value-added times in relation to lead times, nor should it be surprising to see extreme amounts of inventory/WIP. These conditions are systemic to *all* push systems. What is the purpose of doing a VSM with detailed information about the condition of inventory, cycle times and the like at every process if these are already givens in a push system? The point is that just knowing that a push system is used is actionable information. Is the level of detail at each process in a VSM really necessary to know that the system has excessive inventory, lots of delays, and little value-added time in every process? No, of course not.

In using a VSM in this way to see problems, there's an implicit assumption that the root causes are found in the details of the low value-added times, uneven cycle times, and excessive inventory of each process or each process connection. And that a future state map should be done to show what the future should look like and clean up these situations. If each area is addressed and is made to look like the future state map, all is well, right? Viewing this condition from a problem-solving perspective, the push system is the root cause. The information captured in the VSM are the symptoms.

If a VSM is used in this manner, the root cause is not being addressed. And when the root cause is not addressed in problem-solving, countermeasures are ineffective, and the problem remains. This is akin to focusing on the wart on your finger when you have high blood pressure or cancer. The VSM has been very well publicized, such that it's become the shiny object for many in the lean world. A noted author and professor wrote recently about the fact that it's been so well advanced on the lean psyche that "many organizations cannot be convinced that value stream maps are not necessary in order to see waste and improve processes."[6]

In practice, the VSM has become a way to assess the current condition and get some direction on where your focus should be, based on a snapshot in time. Another obvious problem with using a VSM to assess focus is that not all work areas are the same. The nature and type of work being done in one process in the value stream may require more WIP than other areas. Or, due to the layout, distance between processes, size and nature of machines, or number of parts used, one area may have much less value-added time than someplace else.

Conversely, in a pull, or just-in-time, system, production is synchronized and paced. (More on this later.) WIP levels are controlled between and within processes, so that excessive inventories do not exist. Cycle time differences between processes show up as wait time in either the upstream process (the upstream process goes full to the downstream because the downstream is slower. The upstream must wait to build) or the downstream process (because the downstream is faster, the buffer is run out, and the upstream process goes short to the downstream. The downstream must wait on the upstream). In a pull system, either condition is visible.

When pulling, because these problems become visible very quickly, they require action. In other words, it's very easy to understand the difference between the normal and the abnormal, as opposed to a push system. In the case of a buffer between connected processes, too much or too little signals an abnormality. And remember that the buffers between processes can, and likely will, differ from area to area. Is a VSM needed to tell what can clearly be seen?

Not only is there a problem with a tool orientation in the lean world, but there are also problems with the misuse of tools. Let me give an example that's illustrative of what I've encountered over the years.

I was leading a work group to reduce changeover times on a molding machine. We used the Single-Minute Exchange of Dies (SMED) method. One step involves distinguishing those tasks that must be done when the machine is down from those that can be accomplished while the machine is running and minimizing the machine downtime in various ways. For this exercise, the result of our first pass was a reduction from 19+ min per changeover to less than 4 min, a little more than an 80% reduction, or 15 min per changeover. If we had 2 molders × 4 changeovers × 15 min, we would have 120 min/day more production time. Not bad.

Anyway, the far more interesting aspect of the kaizen, to me, was my interaction with the lean consultant. During one of the times he dropped by to give us direction, he said that we needed to use a combination table. I suppose the purpose was to show the time for each work element? I questioned him about why we needed to use that tool. (The combination table is used to show the relationship of the worker to the machines in a process. It's commonly used in a new process set-up during pilot activity, when reducing headcount by combining processes, or when changing the work sequence in processes.) He offered no reasonable answer, and no amount of logic would change his mind. I explained to him it wasn't the right tool and that it would be a waste of time to use it. I guess that was the wrong answer?

First thing the next morning, he arrived at our meeting room with the General Manager in tow. He'd brought it back-up! I was asked again if I was going to use a combination table. I smiled and said, "Sure." After they left, I explained to the group the purpose of the combination table and why this tool was not appropriate. And then we used it. The result was that one member of the group was assigned to map out the time on a series of combination tables. (It took about 3 h.) Since the form is scaled to 105 s (another indication that this was inappropriate tool use), we ended up with a "combination banner." Eleven combination tables were taped end-to-end across the wall with information that we couldn't use. This was a head scratcher. What was going on here?

This SMED activity had been the precursor to the implementation of a Triangle Kanban system that connected batch production to the downstream one-piece flow processes. We had two molding machines that made 42 different part numbers. This was currently being done with schedules at each molder (pushing). Reducing changeover times was the logical first step prior to the Triangle Kanban. Later, on hearing about implementation of the Triangle Kanban, this same consultant asked if I could take him out and explain how this worked. Sure.

These experiences, and others for me, are indicative of the state of our lean world. With very high failure rates, why does this continue? It's hard to understand. I worry that many companies have abandoned lean initiatives or have developed a bad taste. Why would they undertake something that will more than likely fail?

I began to think about why there is so much effort and so little success to show for it. It seems that everyone has a different 10-step or 20-step approach. Or a list of tools that should be used. Or a string of "kaizen events." Successes have been few and far between. But again … why?

As Toyota developed their system through problem-solving and trial and error over the years, there were some bedrock conditions, or elements, that were implemented in their quest to eliminate waste and make "what's needed, when it's needed, in the amount needed." But these elements are being largely ignored in lean transformations. Continuous flow, pull, heijunka, problem-solving, and others are not given the importance they deserve and are often not addressed from a systems perspective. Yet these are requirements for achieving a truly lean production system. As a matter of fact, according to Toyota, "heijunka is a pre-requisite for just-in-time delivery."[7]

Remember,

> Many good companies have respect for individuals, and practice kaizen and other TPS tools ... But what is important is having all the elements together as a system. It must be practiced every day in a very consistent manner, not in spurts.[8]

This statement infers that the individual elements, or tools, are not important without implementation of all the elements, the entire system. Today, we have an advantage that Toyota did not have 70 years ago. We have a history of what happened, the Toyota Template.

At Toyota, we had a saying, "The right process produces the right results." In the following pages, I'll examine the right processes, the order of implementation, and how each contributed to the culture. The failure to follow the Toyota Template, in deference to a tool focus, is the single biggest source of failure of lean initiatives.

The Predicament: Tool emphasis/misuse and heavy reliance on the VSM has led many to address symptoms rather than root causes.

Culture: Culture developed gradually over time because of the template, "having all the elements together as a system ... practiced every day in a very consistent manner, not in spurts."

ENDNOTES

1. Ohno, Taiichi. 1988. *Toyota Production System: Beyond Large-Scale Production,* p. 115. New York, NY: Productivity Press.
2. Baudin, Michel. 2014. Value Stream Mapping, Michel Baudin's Blog. http://michelbaudin.com/tag/value-stream-mapping.
3. Ibid.
4. Ohno, Taiichi. Management and Leadership Quotes, Curious Cat. http://management-quotes.net/authors/Taiichi_Ohno/quote/9692.
5. Ohno, Taiichi. 2013. *Taiichi Ohno's Workplace Management: Special 100th Birthday Edition,* p. 102. New York, NY: McGraw-Hill.
6. Emiliani, Bob. 2017. Wacky Lean House, Bob Emiliani, Innovative lean leadership. www.bobemiliani.com/wacky-lean-house/.
7. Toyota Motor Manufacturing. Toyota production system terms. Georgetown, KY: Toyota. http://toyotaky.com/terms.asp.
8. Liker, Jeffrey K. 2004. *The Toyota Way: 14 Management Principles from the World's Greatest Manufacturer,* p. 27. New York, NY: McGraw-Hill.

3

The Position: Plant First

Our position is where we stand on an issue.

I had the great fortune and wonderful opportunity to work for Toyota Motor Manufacturing—Kentucky in Georgetown, KY for 16 years. I was hired in February, 1988 as a Team Leader and was promoted to Group Leader the following year for the second shift start-up. Looking back, my experience and what I learned has been more valuable than my college degree. It shaped my view of business in general and manufacturing in particular. I view the business world through the lens of my Toyota experience. No apologies.

The motivation for writing a book derives from my personal experiences since leaving Toyota and from what I've read, witnessed, and been told about the failure of so many to develop what's come to be called a "lean" system of their own. One that works for them and is sustainable.

Taiichi Ohno said that "this production system represents a concept in management that will work for any type of business."[1] No question about it. The Toyota Production System (TPS) is the greatest innovation in business management ever. The concepts in TPS are both unique to Toyota and transferable to other businesses. The 7 Wastes, Hoshin Kanri, 8-Step Problem Solving, Continuous Flow, Pull Production, and many others are part of the Toyota system. The discipline to implement and sustain the system across many countries and cultures is a testament to the strength of the TPS. This discipline illustrates Toyota's dedication to their principles.

Ohno said, "I have always firmly believed in the plant first principle … The time that provides me with the most vital information about management is the time I spend in the plant, not in the vice president's office."[2] The plant is the starting point. After all, the plant is where the products are made that are sold. Large amounts of money are made or lost on the production floor. Anyone who's worked on a production floor knows that the coordination required is extremely important. For the trained eye, there is waste everywhere and thus, lots of opportunity for improvement. To me, there is little more interesting than what happens on a production floor in a manufacturing facility. Every day is a learning experience.

That said, sometimes companies also decide to use resources in the office. There's no doubt that there's waste in the office. However, the plant is the customer of the office. As the plant implements improvements, it will naturally pull resources from the office as needed. Changes in support groups will be required as changes are implemented in the plant. These changes are addressed as the pull from the plant, their customer, dictates. Implementing lean in the office simultaneously may not serve a plant first objective. Sometimes, changes in the office silos affect the plant floor adversely. For example, the office could be working on schedule issues while the plant is readying for a pull system. The office should not push change to the floor but should welcome the pull from the plant, as needs arise. Make the conscious decision to focus on a plant first mentality.

A strong production line means a strong business.[3]

The Position: A plant first mentality.

Culture: Focusing on the plant first sends the proper message about the priority of the business. The plant is the key and the reason the business exists.

ENDNOTES

1. Ohno, Taiichi. 1988. *Toyota Production System: Beyond Large-Scale Production*, p. 9. New York, NY: Productivity Press.
2. Ibid., p. 20.
3. Ibid., p. 102.

4

The Purpose: Will and Skill

A purpose is something worthwhile or meaningful that we want to attain.

What I've commonly heard over the years about the Toyota Production System (TPS) goes something like this: "We're not a car company!" "Our product is unique." "We're different. This won't work in our business." "It sounds good but it'll never work here." "We're high mix-low volume so this doesn't apply to us." This is not the way to start a lean initiative. These excuses remind me of something my mama used to tell me, "Can't never could."

> The extent to which we achieve success is dictated by the degree to which management is committed to innovative change, not making excuses.[1]

Lean starts and stops at the top. It does not matter how enthusiastic anyone else in the organization is about waste elimination or lean manufacturing. If the leader is not bent this way, any efforts are a waste of time. Senior leaders must be "committed to innovative change." Talking about it, meeting about it, discussing it at lunch is not enough. Senior leaders should be committed like the pig, not the chicken. (The chicken supplies the eggs. The chicken is involved. The pig furnishes the bacon. The pig is committed!) Employees see through a lack of commitment easily. This means you must change the way you view your position and your daily work. We had a saying at Toyota, "Leaders are teachers." Leaders must become teachers. You must get down in the weeds with everyone else. Participate enthusiastically. Lead! If you do, employee respect and buy-in are greatly improved, and you may learn something too. Lead, and your employees will follow.

[I]f the presidents isolate themselves in, say, their downtown offices, they will fail to stay informed about front-line, or workplace, conditions. This will hamper their ability for effective decision-making.[2]

In defense of senior leaders, I can understand the hesitance to reveal that you may not know much about lean or Toyota. There's a lot of static in the lean world. Unless you worked at Toyota or maybe a supplier for a considerable period of time, it would be impossible to understand TPS, except in an academic way. This is because you were not exposed to the culture. To many leaders, revealing a lack of knowledge might be considered a sign of weakness. Leaders might be a little hesitant to let that fact be known. Most achieved their current position based on their past performance, and that's to be applauded. But the Toyota Template is radically different from traditional manufacturing. Eliminating waste and being efficient are good for your company, your employees, and your community. There is no downside. Leaders should swallow their pride, check their ego at the office door, and get in the mix.

Besides lack of knowledge, another real issue for senior leaders to overcome is the satisfaction that comes with a "marriage to mediocrity." This is the unspoken issue whereby improvement is desired, generally in sales and pricing, but not in areas where it's believed there's risk to the status quo. Oh, they might submit to some kaizen events in specific areas, but nothing of lasting consequence. After all, the company is making money. The current Key Performance Indicators (KPIs) are in reach. Everyone is getting a nice bonus. In this case, leaders do not see a compelling benefit in rocking the boat. This is especially true when they consider the failure rate. After all, the chances of success are historically abysmal. In this case, leaders tend to go through the motions or make a half-hearted commitment. There is no burning desire for change. Why would senior leaders want to change? They see no need. They're happy with the status quo. The tragedy is what's being missed.

Progress cannot be generated when we are satisfied with existing situations.[3]

Thinking about commitment reminds me of an encounter I had in the mid-1990s with a Toyota executive. It happened one Saturday morning. I had come in to the plant with a few of my team members to work on a kaizen project. After the team got started, I went to the break room for a few minutes to do some paperwork. As I was sitting at my desk, one of the doors to the break room flew open. When I looked up, I recognized the president of TMMK (Toyota Motor Manufacturing—KY). He was decked out in Kevlar sleeves and gloves, and he came directly to my desk. A bit surprised, I stood immediately, and we extended our arms to shake hands. As we did, he asked me what I was doing there on a Saturday. I told him that we were working on a kaizen. He said, "Ohhh, thank you very much!" And out the door he went, leaving me to make sense of what had just happened. What was he doing in Body Weld early on a Saturday morning? Did the president of TMMK really need to be at work on a Saturday morning visiting the plant floor? Would anyone have known, or cared, if he weren't? Of course not. He was there, in my view, to encourage our efforts. He was all in. He understood the importance and symbolism of his efforts. This is an example of leadership, and it made a big impression on me. As a senior leader at your business, can you commit yourself to this level of leadership? Do you really have the will?

By the way, this former TMMK president's name is on U.S. Patent # 4,802,616.[4] This is the patent for the Global Body Line (GBL) at Toyota. The GBL (or as we called it, "the blue sky project") was a revolutionary change from the already industry-leading Flexible Body Line (FBL). With the FBL, each model type required three different pallets. This required more pallets traveling from the sub-assembly areas to the Framing Body Line and thus, more traffic lanes in the overhead area. The GBL reduced this need to one interchangeable pallet, which reduced the total number of pallets in use and opened up the overhead area (thus, "the blue sky project"). Additionally, the new pallets held the body panels from inside the shell body, freeing up room for additional robot welding. The GBL was a tremendous advantage for Toyota. The following are some of the benefits of the GBL to Toyota:

30% reduced time vehicle spends in body shop
70% time reduction for major model change
50% cost reduction to add/switch models
50% initial investment reduction
50% assembly footprint reduction
50% lower energy usage
50% maintenance costs reduction[5]

In addition to will, the other aspect of the purpose of the template is skill. Skill means a deep understanding of Toyota's culture, concepts, and critical conditions. This is different from understanding definitions or the purpose of the tools. This understanding means the ability to both teach and do. Ohno said, "To understand is to be able to do."[6] Teaching is the easier part. Numerous lean folks can talk about the tools used by Toyota in addition to many non-Toyota tools. Herein lies one of the contributors to failure. The water has been muddied quite a bit over the years, and there's been no focus. Some classroom work is needed, but the real issue with the skill part is finding someone who both deeply understands, *and* can implement the concepts. I agree with the author of *The Toyota Way*. The best resource is someone with the Toyota DNA, meaning that experience directly from Toyota, or from a company closely linked to them, is best.[7] Of course, I'm biased because Toyota was my personal experience, but the logical thinking is that you want someone who's lived in this culture if you intend to create a similar one. For example, how would someone understand the need for and use of the Triangle kanban if they'd never seen or used it? Given the current odds of success, it makes sense to err on the side of caution. Look for people who have this DNA, who have a strong understanding, and the chances for success are increased.

I want to touch on the cultural aspect briefly. For our purposes, *culture is defined as the characteristics, such as behaviors and beliefs, that are common to an organization.* There's been extensive talk about culture change in the lean community. There are four basic steps, three essential elements, lists of expected behaviors, XX essential lean tools, and on and on. Maybe these concepts are true, but the real issue is *how* to change the culture. Remember, Ohno didn't set out to form a culture. His direction was to catch up with America in 3 years. Toyota was working on becoming an efficient and profitable automaker. The result of the systems and concepts that they adopted over time formed the culture. This is an extremely important point. The Toyota culture happened, over time, because of the things done and taught by Ohno and company.

Why is this culture difficult to achieve? Maybe, if we look back at the words of Mr. Ohno, we'll find a clue. After 1962, Toyota was attempting to expand the kanban system to their outside suppliers. These outside firms were invited to Toyota to see the system and to study it up close.

Ohno said, "This way of teaching gave us the ability to demonstrate an efficient production method in an actual production plant. As a matter of fact, *they would have had difficulty understanding the system without seeing it in action.*"[8] Could it be that this difficulty exists today? How many have not seen the system in action? If I wanted to be a major league baseball pitcher, I could be shown how to grip a circle change, how to wind up, given points on leverage, and so on. I could put on a uniform and trot out to the mound. I might be moderately conversant in baseball lingo and strategy. I could even chew a plug of tobacco. Would this make me a major league pitcher? Of course not. It would require years of training under knowledgeable coaches along with many hours of practice and real game situations. The same applies to TPS. Reading about it and talking about it are not the same as actually living it and doing it.

Is TPS truly understood?

The Purpose: A strong will at the top of the organization combined with the skill to implement.

Culture: Commitment at the top communicates and demonstrates the importance of the culture change. Leaders lead. The skill is acquired initially and taught/learned through the organization.

ENDNOTES

1. Ohno, Taiichi. 1988. *Just-in-Time for Today and Tomorrow*, p. xii. Cambridge, MA: Productivity Press.
2. Ibid., p. 77.
3. Ohno, Taiichi. Inspiring Quotes. www.inspiringquotes.us/quotes/BcJU_NjI3MyDd.
4. Naruse et al. 'System for positioning automotive vehicle side body.' United States, 1989. http://pdfpiw.uspto.gov/.piw?Docid=4802616&idkey=NONE&homeurl=http%3A%252F%252Fpatft.uspto.gov%252Fnetahtml%252FPTO%252Fpatimg.htm
5. Adapted from Visnic, Bill. 2002. Toyota adopts new flexible assembly system. Wards Auto. November 1. http://wardsauto.com/news-analysis/toyota-adopts-new-flexible-assembly-system.
6. Ohno, Taiichi. 2013. *Taiichi Ohno's Workplace Management, Special 100th Birthday Edition*, p. 174. New York, NY: McGraw-Hill.
7. Liker, Jeffrey K. 2004.*The Toyota Way, 14 Management Principles from the World's Greatest Manufacturer*, p. 294. New York, NY: McGraw-Hill.
8. Ohno, Taiichi. 1988. *Toyota Production System: Beyond Large-Scale Production*, p. 34. New York, NY: Productivity Press.

5

The Plan: Hoshin Kanri

A plan is a detailed method or process to achieve an end.

Changing the culture begins with a plan to do it. This is one difference from what Ohno did during his years driving waste elimination. He may have done so, but it doesn't appear that he worked off an organized plan. Either way, today we can make plans knowing the history of Ohno's actions at Toyota. Undertaking an overhaul of manufacturing can be seen as a daunting task. Where to start, what to do, and in what order are pertinent questions. Lean efforts have generally concentrated on numerous "kaizen events" in the belief that changing operations through these improvement exercises will, somehow, lead to a lean culture that adds to the bottom line. Some even determine which improvement projects to tackle based on some supposed dollar savings. Possibly sometime down the road this should be considered, but it is not a good idea in the beginning. Where's the problem-solving? The focus is a cost figure, not problem-solving. This approach will change the culture alright, but not in a lean direction. The right plan leads to implementation of the right concepts and methods in the right order.

To improve operations through adoption of the Toyota Template, the plan must be directionally correct regarding the current condition. It over-arches the scope of the change and addresses shortcomings. It's been said that a goal without a plan is just a wish. Most companies have some sort of annual planning process; however, the template uses the Hoshin Kanri method. Hoshin Kanri simply means policy deployment. This method is unique in that it aligns goals with the company mission as well as with the annual objectives up, down, and across the organization at every level. This planning process is critical to organizational alignment.

The Hoshin plan acts as the rudder for the business. It keeps all areas moving in the same direction. It involves everyone from the executive suite to the floor level in all departments. The yearly planning should begin taking shape several months prior to the next fiscal year. The planning process to achieve alignment takes some time, and you need to be well prepared to begin implementation from the beginning. The yearly plan should align with your long-term strategy.

Alignment begins at the senior level. They're responsible for the objectives of the enterprise. They should be looking 3 to 5 years ahead strategically in broad terms. Where do you want to be in the future? Narrow goals will become simply projects to complete, which stymies participation. Of course, these should follow the S.M.A.R.T. acronym (Specific, Measurable, Achievable, Realistic, and Time-targeted). Some examples might be to reduce overall costs by 20% or increase customer satisfaction by 25% over the time frame; whatever is suitable for your current condition.

After agreement on these broad objectives at the senior level, each one is broken down based on the time frame. For example, using the 20% reduction in overall costs over years, you could simply set the yearly goal at 5% per year. This shouldn't be automatic, however. There could be circumstances that dictate that the goal is 8% for the first year and 3% for each of the next 4 years. Senior leaders should consider all relevant factors to determine achievable and realistic goals.

Each department level then determines their tactics to achieve their goals. These should be developed with the approval of upper-level management, so that there is agreement that the selected actions support the upper-level goals. This is called *catchball*, with the idea being that these actions are passed up and down the management hierarchy so that there is agreement on alignment. For example, each vice president might meet with each of their direct reports and agree on the tactics. Once the tactics are determined and agreed on, they should be reviewed at regular intervals to determine whether you're making progress or not. During the review, decisions are made as to whether the progress is acceptable and any adjustments that need to be made.

The production floor is where the tactics become operational. Floor leaders must work out the details to support the tactics. This is where the rubber hits the road. Again, catchball is done between department heads and floor management to ensure that the operational part of the plan aligns with the department goals. All this planning can be illustrated using a tool called the X-Matrix. This visual shows how the plans are correlated, how they support the objectives, and the expected impacts.

There are several benefits of Hoshin Kanri planning. It focuses the organization on common goals, involves leaders in the planning and communication of the goals, and holds leaders responsible for their respective parts of the plan. It ensures that the company's goals are being driven at all levels of the organization. It helps to dilute silo thinking and supports prioritization of resources in support of the goals. Hoshin Kanri is a systematic approach to planning.

Following the Toyota Template will dictate, in the beginning, what goals should be included. These will be critical goals of the planning process up front. Concepts such as problem-solving and waste recognition education, continuous flow, a pull system, standard work, and heijunka could be front and center in an initial Hoshin Kanri plan. The plan always starts from the current condition.

As with any plan, we must have ways to measure success. Key Productivity Indicators (KPIs) are used to measure progress toward goal attainment. KPIs should exist at every level of the management team. They're tracked regularly at the appropriate intervals – daily, weekly, monthly, and so on – depending on the place where they're used. Here are the rules for KPIs:

KPI RULES

Must be in control of owner: For example, is man hours/unit under the control of the supervisor at the floor level, or is staffing determined further up the chain of command? Wrong or missing parts are a more appropriate measure. Or maybe non-production overtime hours? These are in the span of control of the floor supervisor.

Must drive desired behaviors: For example, overall equipment effectiveness at the floor level can drive poor decisions by making products not needed so as to meet the KPI. Downtime is a good measure: how many should be made vs. how many were made.

Must be actionable information that drives improvement: Can you clearly see the gap between the current condition and the goal? Measure the actual against the goal.

Must be aligned with the overall strategy: Does the KPI drive behaviors that support the corporate objectives? For example, the corporate goal may be to increase customer satisfaction. The plant may measure On-Time-Delivery (OTD) in support of the corporate goal to improve customer satisfaction. The plant departments may measure off-line repairs as a KPI to support OTD, while the work group may measure wrong/missing parts in support of reducing off-line repairs. The idea is that missing parts contribute to off-line repairs, which affect OTD, which in turn, affects customer satisfaction. Logically, when the process minimizes missing parts, the plant's off-line repair KPI will improve, OTD increases, and customer satisfaction is higher. The KPIs are aligned up and down the organization, and wrong/missing parts are in the control of the supervisor.

Minimize the number of KPIs: Measure only those things that affect the goals. Don't measure everything!

Measuring Overall Progress

I'm not aware of any measure that's accepted by everyone, but one KPI that is a good indication of relative leanness, or efficiency, is Inventory Turnover.

$$\text{Inventory Turnover} = \frac{\text{Cost of Goods Sold}}{\text{Average Inventory}}$$

This is a KPI that, when measured over time, can indicate progress in increasing efficiency. By turning inventory faster, it is possible to significantly reduce the amount of inventory on the floor. The money previously tied up in inventory is now cash in the bank and can be used for other things.

Another measure that is sometimes used is Days Inventory Outstanding (DIO). It's just the opposite of Inventory Turnover. The math is:

$$\text{Days Inventory Outstanding (DIO)} = \frac{\text{Inventory level for the period}}{\text{Average sales per day for the period}}$$

What it says is that for every dollar of goods sold, there is a dollar amount of inventory in the system. So, if the average sales revenue per day is $2 million and the average inventory is $50 million, then the DIO is 25. With this measure, the lower the DIO, the better off you are, because the daily sales figure is achieved with less inventory.

This focus on uniting everyone toward a common purpose and valuing the importance of each person's role through Hoshin Kanri brings the organization together. It creates a common vision that is not only shared with everyone in the organization but requires the involvement of leadership at all levels in the formulation of plans at each respective level. A sense of teamwork evolves out of the input from all levels and areas of the organization in pursuit of common goals. This plan will align and unite the enterprise.

The Plan: The Hoshin plan is the method to align the organization.
Culture: The Hoshin plan lays the groundwork for culture change by valuing every leader's input, supporting common goals, and instilling a sense of teamwork through the organization.

6

The Property: Waste Elimination

A property is a characteristic common to everyone in a particular class or group.

> The preliminary step toward application of the Toyota Production System is to identify wastes completely.[1]
>
> Eliminating waste must be a business's first objective.[2]
>
> The fundamental doctrine of the Toyota Production System is the total elimination of waste.[3]

The property is the essential attribute shared by all members of a group. In the case of a lean culture, that essential attribute is the understanding of waste, how to identify it in the work environment, and its continuous elimination. Ohno addressed this topic at considerable length and said that it was the "fundamental doctrine of the Toyota Production System."[4]

The best method to understand waste is to go to the worksite, the gemba, and begin identifying waste by observing the work. The story goes that Taiichi Ohno would stand an engineer in a chalk circle drawn on the shop floor. His direction would be: "Watch the process." Ohno would return later and ask the engineer, "What do you see?" Ohno wanted them to learn to see what he saw. So, if the reply was something other than what Ohno had seen, he would leave the engineer to "watch some more."[5] This tactic continued until the manager saw the same problems Ohno had seen.

The way I think about this in my mind is what I call *straight line thinking*. As we know, the shortest distance between two points is a straight line. I look at value streams and the processes that make them up from the viewpoint of a straight line. Observing the activities in a process is about how to make the process as straight, figuratively, as possible. From this viewpoint, the activities that cause this line to be crooked are highlighted. Straightening out the line by eliminating or mitigating those activities is the goal.

> All we are doing is looking at the time line, from the moment the customer gives us an order to the point when we collect the cash. And we are reducing the time line by removing the non-value added wastes.[6]

Over time, and through practice, this awareness becomes ingrained in your thinking, and you will become sensitive to waste—even away from work in your leisure time. Mr. Ohno started with the notion that waste should be identified. He defined seven wastes in a way that was easy to understand.

Learning about the seven types of waste happened very early in my training at Toyota (prior to the addition of an eighth waste). During new hire orientation in the classroom, we were introduced to the concept, examples were given, and there was much discussion as we tried to understand this thinking. I'd never thought about work in this way before. It seemed a little simplistic at first, but it made good sense. This understanding was a key piece of my early training in the Toyota Production System philosophy. I believe it's an important concept, both because of the emphasis placed on waste illustrated by Ohno's chalk circle example and also due to the emphasis placed on the concept in my experience at Toyota. In a similar fashion, I too learned by "standing in the chalk circle" in my daily work at the gemba.

> The most important objective of the Toyota system has been to increase production efficiency by consistently and thoroughly eliminating waste.[7]

OHNO'S 7 WASTES

Overproduction

Manufacture of products in advance or in excess of demand. This wastes money, time, and space. And too early is the same as too much. Overproduction is understood to be the worst waste, because it leads to other wastes such as waiting, transportation, and excessive inventory.

Overproduction both *hides* waste and *creates* additional waste. This leads to unnecessary costs. More work-in-process than is necessary can result in storage and labor costs associated with storing and searching for parts.

More people, more equipment, and more floor space are needed. This can be hard to see because of the constant activity around the inventory. More people doing stuff ... moving, storing, and searching looks like work, but it's not. There's no value-added to the product in these activities. It's simply movement, and not all movement is work. Given the need for extra people, more equipment, and the excessive inventory, the need may arise for a warehouse. In this case, additional workers and equipment would be required to staff the warehouse and transport inventory to and from it.

There is no waste in business more terrible than overproduction.[8]

Waiting

Many times, especially in a push environment, this waste is difficult to see. One of the realities of push systems is that there's a tendency to accumulate items not needed, and plenty of them, while the items actually needed are not present. When this situation exists, what's made is what can be made, not what should be made. Workers make something to stay busy and productive. This can make it very difficult to see wait time in a process. The time that should have shown up as wait time is taken up with making something not needed at the time.

In any manufacturing situation, we frequently see people working ahead. Instead of waiting, the worker works on the next job, so the waiting is hidden.[9]

Another instance is when the work is not balanced between two connected processes. This is easier to see in a pull system. When the downstream process is faster than the upstream process, the downstream process waits for the next part. It's also easier to see when the processes are in close proximity. If there is a buffer between the processes, then the buffer will run dry over time. A common countermeasure, in lieu of properly addressing the imbalance, is to work the slower upstream process for a longer period of time to build up a buffer. Usually this is accomplished with overtime. Or sometimes, additional workers are added to keep up.

Transportation

Excessive movement of products. There is a certain amount of transportation that's necessary. Work that is necessary, but adds no value, is called *auxiliary work*. By creating flow from process to process, even the seemingly necessary transporting of parts can be minimized. This is similar to the thinking that is used in a Single-Minute Exchange of Dies activity when minimizing the time the machine is down. Gravity-fed rollers and conveyors between connected processes can help.

In situations that require equipment such as forklifts to move parts between processes due to distance, size of the part, or the need to transport small quantities, commonizing containers so that they're stackable and pairing up deliveries based on a common area can significantly reduce the waste of transportation. There are other ways to reduce excess transporting of parts (such as electronic call systems), but I won't address them here.

Over-Processing

Doing more than is necessary or more than the customer is willing to pay for. This happens sometimes when work has been added to the process in the past but is no longer needed. A deburr process could be an example, when the source of the burr has been successfully countermeasured upstream but has not been communicated to the folks doing the deburring.

Another example is when an unnecessary repair is done. A part with a small dent in it that's used in the underbody of a car, is never visible to the customer, and doesn't affect the integrity of the part doesn't require repair. To do a repair in this circumstance would be over-processing.

We regard only work that is needed as real work and define the rest as waste.[10]

Excessive Inventory

Excess inventory is an unneeded safety blanket in manufacturing. One of the sources of excess inventory occurs when processes are separated by distance from their internal customers. When processes are separated, the need arises for a buffer between them, because one-piece flow is not possible due to this separation. The trick is to determine the minimal buffer size and establish a standard quantity. The rule of thumb for a buffer is the smallest amount needed to keep the downstream process running smoothly and consistently. After this quantity is determined, the process must be disciplined to stop producing when the buffer is full. The temptation, due to the distance, is to fill up the space. Excessive inventory hides problems, relaxes the sense of urgency, and wastes resources through costs of transporting, storage, and maintenance.

This type of hoarding, however, is no longer practical. Industrial society must develop the courage, or rather common sense, to produce only what is needed, when it is needed and in the amount needed.[11]

Unnecessary Motion

There are two issues associated with unnecessary motion. First is the effect on the worker. Excessive motion can be tiring both physically and mentally. Second is the time element. Extra walk time is not productive; it's merely moving. Unnecessary motion can be applied to equipment, too. Excessive motion in equipment can hasten wear and tear, resulting in downtime.

> Worker movement in the production area must be working, or value-added movement. Moving is not necessarily working. Working means actually advancing the process toward completing the job."[12]

Defects

Rework/remake, inspecting, sorting, and quarantining inventory take time and cost money.

> Regardless of how much is said, adopting the Toyota System will be meaningless without a complete understanding of the elimination of waste.[13]

> Unless we change how we think, there is a limit to what we can accomplish by continuing our same thinking.[14]

5S

5S is a systematic method to identify and eliminate waste and keep the workplace safe, clean, and organized. One of the important results of good 5S is the elimination of waste. 5S is a relatively new term. When I started at Toyota, the term was 4S. Seiri, Seiton, Seiso, and Seiketsu were the original terms. The 5th S, Shitsuke (self-discipline or sustain), was added somewhere along the way. Many times, the meaning of 5S is to clean up, straighten up, label items, shadow box things, designate locations, and so on; however, 5S is much more than a cleaning activity. 5S is a discipline that sets the stage for other elements such as standard work and Total Productive Maintenance. To implement a good 5S program, the steps should be done in order and one at a time. This is also the best way to teach others.

Start with Seiri, or sift and sort. In this first step, we separate the most important items from the least important and isolate the least important things outside the work area. The least important items are either discarded or red-tagged and placed in a designated area temporarily. Establish rules around how long items are kept in the red tag area before being discarded. More than once, I've fished out items left in the red tag area by another group that I could use. Many times, we found numerous duplicate items that we used, such as a battery or air guns, that we'd stored somewhere and forgotten about. Seems like we always found extra tip-changing tools. The most important items are things that are used regularly: items that, when you need them, you need them now. You can separate the items by frequency of use. This is what you do when you have a garage sale. Separate what you want from what you don't want. Some of it you discard, and some of it you sell. A key learning from Seiri is that you can accumulate a lot of stuff if you're not well organized. This should illustrate to those involved how wasteful disorganization can be. This is a point of emphasis. Complete Seiri before you begin the next step.

The second "S" is Seiton, or set in order. These important items should have designated locations that are visible and labeled. Why label it? So you know what's missing when it's not there. For tools, this can also be accomplished with shadowing. Another way is to make the location only workable for a specific tool, so that nothing else can go there. Round peg, round hole thinking. Logically, these items are kept in a convenient and ergonomically appropriate place for the user. The user should decide the best locations, as they use these items regularly. Be consistent in the way you store and label items from process to process. Complete Seiton before you begin the next step.

Seiso, or as we called it "spick and span," is the third step. After getting rid of items not needed and setting in order items that are needed, the next step is to give the area a good cleaning. Determine, for each process, what this means. Some areas may require some type of specific cleaning not required in others. This is a good opportunity to find and identify problems within the process, especially those that seem to have become accepted as normal. The source of problems such as water, oil, or air leaks can be determined and addressed. Complete Seiso before you begin the next step.

These first three steps establish the standard. Now that the area is straightened and cleaned, it should be maintained. Seiketsu, or standardization, is next. A task list should be assigned to each process, clearly defining expectations, including when each task should be accomplished. A sign-off box may also be included on the list, which is a reminder for the worker to complete each task and a way for the leader to follow up. Again, there may be similarities between processes, but be aware of specific problems in each area. And those water and oil leak sources can be included in the standardization of the process 5S checklist.

The last "S" is Shitsuke, or sustaining and improving the condition. This can be accomplished with periodic audits. The grading should be strict. Challenge each area to improve their process each audit. The 5S process is a discipline, both on the floor and elsewhere. And frankly, this should be something that each area takes pride in daily. Treat the work area as if it were your home. But this home is inhabited by numerous people, and many others can view the living conditions. Furthermore, the work area reflects the people's work, and it's easily compared with the neighbors in the process next door. In this case, peer pressure is a good thing. Generally, when expectations are high, people step up to the challenge.

The condition of production areas is the first thing I notice in a plant. One can tell a lot about how the plant is running by the 5S condition on the plant floor. If production leadership cannot establish and maintain an organized work area, what would make anyone believe that there's discipline in other areas such as safety or quality? If we can't keep the house clean, what else is not working well?

5S should be understood early, as it relates directly to waste elimination. It's very important to create and maintain an exceptional condition. This, however, can be a bit challenging in a push system of production. The general chaos in push systems can make it difficult to focus on 5S due to the amount of time required to deal with the problems associated with push, particularly the excess WIP in the processes. After the implementation of pull, the excess WIP goes away, and it's easier to accomplish a good condition.

As stated at the beginning of the chapter, waste elimination is the "fundamental doctrine of the Toyota Production System" and is the goal for all members. It provides a common way for everyone to view their work. Further, by challenging employees to be open to better ways to perform their work and by being accepting of their ideas, mutual respect is enhanced between individuals and work groups. This is their shared "fundamental doctrine."

Working through this lens will help you to begin to understand your inefficiencies. When you begin to view work with waste in mind, many ideas will come to mind. You will question why many activities are done. Think of the straight line. Through observations in the workplace, you will start to wonder why. Why do we do this or that? And further, you will begin to ask why not. It will challenge you to look at your processes in a different way, a waste-conscious way. When you do, your eyes will open, and your mind will wonder about the possibilities. Developing the understanding of waste and becoming acutely sensitive to it is critical to building a lean culture.

The Property: Deep understanding of waste and making elimination the first objective.

Culture: The commitment to the "fundamental doctrine" of the elimination of waste instills a common discipline about what is acceptable and what is not. This discipline, established through a strong 5S program, sets the foundation for discipline in other areas, such as quality.

ENDNOTES

1. Ohno, Taiichi. 1988. *Toyota Production System: Beyond Large-Scale Production,* p. 19. New York, NY: Productivity Press.
2. Ibid., p. 129.
3. Ohno, Taiichi. 1988. *Just-in-Time for Today and Tomorrow,* p. 1. Cambridge, MA: Productivity Press.
4. Ibid.
5. Liker, Jeffrey K. 2004. *The Toyota Way: 14 Management Principles from the World's Greatest Manufacturer,* p. 216. New York, NY: McGraw-Hill.
6. Ohno, Taiichi. 1988. *Toyota Production System: Beyond Large-Scale Production,* p. 9. New York, NY: Productivity Press.
7. Ibid., p. 13.
8. Ibid., p. 14.
9. Ibid., p. 59.
10. Ibid., p. 19.
11. Ibid., p. 15.
12. Ibid., p. 58.
13. Ibid, p. 56.
14. Ohno, Taiichi. 2013. *Taiichi Ohno's Workplace Management: Special 100th Birthday Edition,* p. 18. New York, NY: McGraw-Hill.

7

The Practice: Standard Work

To practice is to repeat something over and over to become proficient.

> Sometime in 1937–1938, my boss at Toyoda Spinning and Weaving told me to prepare standard work methods for textile work. It was a difficult project.[1]

> A proper work procedure cannot be written from a desk. It must be tried and revised many times in the production plant. Furthermore, it must be a procedure that anybody can understand.[2]

> My first move as the manager of the machining shop was to introduce standardized work.[3]

Taiichi Ohno arrived at Toyota Motors from the loom business, where he had experience with standard work. He developed his method in the loom business beginning with a book that he bought. Having worked through this "difficult project" with only a textbook, he was well aware of the benefits derived from standard work. He was told to do it. It wasn't done, as far as we know, for any reason other than that he was told to do it.

At Toyota, the standard work sheet contains three elements:

1. Cycle time
2. Work sequence
3. Standard inventory

It's an overview of the work process. Ohno said that standard work "plays an important role in Toyota's visual management system."[4] The standard work is placed at the work station as a visual management tool. This is the way the process is to be done currently, and anyone can see what should be happening. There are many advantages.

The basic premise of standard work is that when the work is performed the same way each time, the result will be consistent. The work cycle will be completed consistently, in the allotted time, discounting other issues, because the work content is the same for each cycle. And the business impact can be large, depending on the number of processes you may have. Consider a simple example. Let's say you make 100 of a product each day, you employ 50 people, and by implementing standard work you can reduce your cycle times by 6 s. 100 products $\times$ 50 people $\times$ 6 s = 30,000 s. That's over 8 hours per day, 1 person, or the equivalent of 2% of your workforce.

In addition to a consistent cycle time, the quality of the product being made will be consistent. Common sense tells us that doing something the same way every time will yield the same results. There are many examples that could be cited from our personal lives. We brush our teeth or shave the same way every time. The results may not be good, but they're the same. By determining the "least waste way" to do something, quality is improved. It also prevents operational errors, again, for the same reason. When the work is routine, accidents become less likely. Ohno enumerates several benefits due to standard work:

> We have eliminated waste by examining available resources, rearranging machines, improving machining processes, installing autonomous systems, improving tools, analyzing transportation methods, and optimizing the amount of materials on hand for machining. High production efficiency has also been maintained by preventing recurrence of defective products, operational mistakes, and accidents, and by incorporating worker's ideas. All of this is possible because of the inconspicuous standard work sheet.[5]

Standard work is a critical part of the Toyota Production System (TPS). Its application is common throughout all areas of Toyota, on the floor and in the office. However, it's important, at this point, to address standard work in the order of events as it relates to the Toyota Template. This was the first order of business for Ohno at Toyota. He'd been charged with catching up with the American auto industry in 3 years. He realized the benefits and had experience with standard work from his loom days. He has said that one cannot improve without first having a standard. All that being said, standard work is not the first step in the template, for a couple of reasons.

Keep in mind that today, we have the advantage of the full picture of the TPS. And we know that standard work was implemented early at Toyota.

However, when producing in a push system, standard work can be challenging. Having lots of what's not needed and none of what's needed, which happens regularly in push systems, creates a difficult environment for implementing and consistently following standard work. It can be written, but it may not be followed. In push systems, products don't sync up when they should. Sometimes, overstaffing is a consequence due to the tendency to staff areas to handle the extreme shifts in production volume. With more people than are really needed, the work content for each worker will be very different than in a pull system.

The point is that if standard work is done prior to implementing a pull system, it will likely result in rewriting much of the standard work. More importantly, even in a push system, there already exists a certain way that products are made. It may not be the best way, but at least there's a currently established method of making products. For these two reasons, (1) there's currently a way products are made, and (2) standard work will change after pull implementation, standard work should be implemented after pull production.

An additional benefit to implementing standard work after implementing pull is that pulling will highlight the bottleneck areas in production. The need for standard work will become apparent when pulling production through the plant. In fact, when pulling first, the bottleneck areas can serve to prioritize the standard work efforts. There will likely be much workload balancing to be done after pulling. This would be the time to routinize the process.

TOTAL PRODUCTIVE MAINTENANCE (TPM) AND MACHINE BACK-UP: TENSION IN THE LINE

> Operational availability is the rate that you can run the machine ... operational availability requires good PM.[6]
>
> People confuse operational availability and rate of operation .... I think this confusion is a result of people feeling that it is a loss to leave the machines idle when they are in an operable condition.[7]

Earlier, in the discussion of waste, the fact that overproduction tends to hide problems was addressed. One of the issues hidden, or made less urgent by inventory, is machine downtime. When machines go down in a push system, the existence of excessive inventory throughout the system covers up many of the machine problems. The downtime may be known, but it may not rise to a level requiring immediate action. Intermittent equipment stops, and sometimes extended stoppages, are covered up by the inventory. This situation tends to cause a more relaxed attitude toward machine downtime on the part of both production and maintenance.

Just-in-time (JIT) production, or pulling, through the plant introduces "tension in the line." Each process feels the tug from its customer for JIT delivery. This is radically different from a push system. When a machine goes down, the impact is felt sooner, and the urgency is greater. Because of this, it becomes more critical for equipment to perform when needed. This tension leads to a heightened sense of urgency with both production and maintenance. A strong partnership between production and maintenance committed to a comprehensive TPM system is critical.

> The right approach to maintenance is to keep your machines and equipment in perfect condition and make repairmen unnecessary.[8]

There is much production can do to contribute to the upkeep of equipment: activities such as regular cleaning and inspection of the equipment, lubrication and fluid checks, loose cables and hoses, routine tightening or simple parts changes, and simply observing machine operations. Like a car that is familiar, the machines become familiar to the users. When they notice a change, or see something abnormal, they should work closely with maintenance by making them aware and helping to assess the situation. Maintenance activities include items such as inspection of areas that are more difficult to see or that may require special equipment, cable and hose changes, and scheduled part replacement or adjustment. An agreed, standardized delineation of responsibilities between production and maintenance is important. There's a lot of information on TPM that can be used to build a great system, such as training programs, equipment building or purchase procedure, managing the spare parts inventory, and so on.

Even with a great maintenance program, all equipment goes down from time to time. Sometimes, the downtime can last for an extended period of time. For this reason, the ability to perform a back-up procedure to keep production going and the line moving is critical. We had a lot of equipment in Body Weld. On just one robot line, with 4 robots per station and 15 stations, there were 60 pieces of equipment that could quit working at any time. With several lines, all the sub-assembly equipment, manual equipment, conveyors, and the like, something was bound to stop running from time to time.

We began early on to develop back-up procedures for as much of the equipment as possible. For each robot, we had a written, detailed back-up. It included information such as the type of welding gun, illustrated weld locations, the number of people required to perform the back-up, and where to do it. Each was developed to perform in TAKT (The time that should be taken to produce something.) time. Since we were using different equipment to do the welding, quality was an important consideration. The back-up procedure must produce an acceptable level of quality as close to the original condition as possible.

TEAMWORK: THE MULTI-SKILLED EMPLOYEE

As an experiment, I arranged the various machines in the sequence of the machining process. This was a radical change from the conventional system …. We encountered strong resistance among the production workers, however, even though there was no increase in work or hours. Our craftsmen did not like the new arrangement requiring them to function as multi-skilled operators.[9]

Ohno encountered resistance when he did his experiment because it threatened the status quo of workers who'd always been craftsmen, operating one machine only. His desire was that workers would operate more than one machine, as had been accomplished in the loom business. This was made possible with autonomation, giving human judgment to machines. This use of autonomation brought about the multi-skilled worker at Toyota.

[T]raining and assigning operators to handle multiple jobs was essential to the flexibility required on flow-based production lines.[10]

Along with the multi-skilled worker came the need for more intensive training. Now, the operators had responsibility for several machines. Standard work became even more important. In addition, this multi-skilled notion spread to several processes, each with several machines. Workers began to learn to operate multiple pieces of equipment and later to rotate from process to process during the workday. This highlighted the need for more and better training.

No goal, regardless of how small, can be achieved without adequate training.[11]

To this end, Toyota uses the Training Within Industry (TWI) methods. TWI is a detailed training method developed by the U.S. Army at the beginning of World War II. The problem in America was that many able-bodied men who were working in manufacturing were leaving the work force, voluntarily or involuntarily, to fight in the war. At the same time as the experienced work force was leaving, the government was requiring manufacturing to accelerate for the needs of the war effort. Manufacturing was hit from both sides. Experienced workers left as production was increasing. This created a big problem for the United States and industry in particular.

The training program consists of three modules, sometimes called the "Js." They are Job Instruction (JI), Job Methods (JM), and Job Relations (JR). They're very detailed, step-by-step instructions for how to train a new worker on a job. A thorough training program was needed, and the Army provided it. This was also a time when many women began to work outside the home to replace their husband's income. Remember "Rosie the Riveter"? Many single women also entered the labor pool as demand was increasing. There's a lot of detail that I won't address here, but suffice it to say that the program worked very well.

After the war, the United States began assisting Japan and Europe in rebuilding their economics, and this training migrated across both ponds. Eventually, Toyota adopted TWI and still uses it to this day, particularly the Job Instruction module. I remember taking classes in JI, JR, and JM and being coached to follow the methods to the letter. The detail is such that it includes things like "set the worker at ease" and asking "what do you know about this process?" I was given small, laminated cards with the steps to each module that I kept in my pocket calendar for a long time to help me remember. TWI is the critical piece in the training of multi-skilled workers at Toyota.

In addition to the TWI training methods, a break-in period was developed for training new or transfer team members on a new process. In Body Weld, we used a 4-week break-in period. Each process was broken down into parts. The member was trained on Part 1 first. And then, within Part 1 training, we'd ramp up a little at a time. For example, Part 1 might consist of picking up the piece, welding three nuts on it, and placing it into a multi-welder. The training might call for the member to do 1-in-3 for the first 2 hours of their training. The next 2-hour period would call for them to do 2-in-3. Then, the third period would call for 3-in-3. The next phase would involve teaching Part 2 of the process in the same manner. After learning Parts 1 and 2, they'd be required to do them together, maybe 1-in-3, and so on. Figure 7.1 shows an example of a training break-in schedule.

Hour	Monday	Tuesday	Wednesday	Thursday	Friday
1	Process 1 - Part 1 — 1 of 4	Process 1 - Part 2 — 1 of 4	Process 1 - Part 3 — 1 of 4	Process 1 - Part 4 — 1 of 4	Process 1 - Parts 1, 2, 3, and 4 — 2 of 4
2	Process 1 - Part 1 — 1 of 4	Process 1 - Part 2 — 1 of 4	Process 1 - Part 3 — 2 of 4	Process 1 - Part 2 — 2 of 4	Process 1 - Parts 1, 2, 3, and 4 — 2 of 4
3	Process 1 - Part 1 — 2 of 4	Process 1 - Part 2 — 2 of 4	Process 1 - Part 3 — 2 of 4	Process 1 - Part 4 — 3 of 4	Process 1 - Parts 1, 2, 3, and 4 — 3 of 4
4	Process 1 - Part 1 — 2 of 4	Process 1 - Part 2 — 3 of 4	Process 1 - Part 3 — 3 of 4	Process 1 - Part 4 — 4 of 4	Process 1 - Parts 1, 2, 3, and 4 — 3 of 4
5	Process 1 - Part 1 — 3 of 4	Process 1 - Part 2 — 3 of 4	Process 1 - Part 3 — 4 of 4	Process 1 - Part 4 — 4 of 4	Process 1 - Parts 1, 2, 3, and 4 — 4 of 4
6	Process 1 - Part 1 — 3 of 4	Process 1 - Part 2 — 4 of 4	Process 1 - Parts 1, 2, and 3 — 2 of 4	Process 1 - Parts 1, 2, 3, and 4 — 2 of 4	Process 1 - Parts 1, 2, 3, and 4 — 4 of 4
7	Process 1 - Part 1 — 4 of 4	Process 1 - Parts 1 and 2 — 2 of 4	Process 1 - Parts 1, 2, and 3 — 2 of 4	Process 1 - Parts 1, 2, 3, and 4 — 2 of 4	Process 1 - Parts 1, 2, 3, and 4 — 4 of 4
8	Review SOS. Confirm understanding. Ask if any questions. Explain next day's plan.	Review SOS. Confirm understanding. Ask if any questions. Explain next day's plan.	Review SOS. Confirm understanding. Ask if any questions. Explain next day's plan.	Review SOS. Confirm understanding. Ask if any questions. Explain next day's plan.	Review SOS. Confirm understanding. Ask if any questions. Explain next work assignment.
Trainer Sign/Date					
T/M Sign/Date					

FIGURE 7.1

Break-in training schedule example.

After the 4-week period, the member could perform the entire job in TAKT time, on their own. This method served a couple of purposes. It allowed the member to become accustomed to the pace gradually, which was much safer and resulted in better quality. It also allowed the member to become comfortable handling the parts and learning with minimal stress. Additionally, any quality checks could be more easily learned. The trainer was present to assist and to answer questions or show them any knack they'd learned through experience that might be helpful.

The Practice: Establish standard work in all areas, including production, maintenance, and training.

Culture: The establishment of standard work in all areas builds the culture by demonstrating respect for all employees through acceptance of input from those doing the work, by setting attainable and agreed-on expectations, and by systematically eliminating waste. Standard work is well defined, sets a reasonable work pace, and is safe. The TWI method demonstrates the importance of training. TPM requires teamwork between maintenance and production in keeping machines functional.

ENDNOTES

1. Ohno, Taiichi. 1988. *Toyota Production System: Beyond Large-Scale Production*, p. 20. New York, NY: Productivity Press.
2. Ibid.
3. Shimokawa, Koichi, and Fujimoto, Takahiro. 2009. *The Birth of Lean*, p. 8. Cambridge, MA: The Lean Enterprise Institute.
4. Ohno, Taiichi. 1988. *Toyota Production System: Beyond Large-Scale Production*, p. 22. New York, NY: Productivity Press.
5. Ibid., p. 21.
6. Ohno, Taiichi. 2013. *Taiichi Ohno's Workplace Management: Special 100th Birthday Edition*, p. 121. New York, NY: McGraw-Hill.
7. Ibid, p. 122.
8. Shimokawa, Koichi, and Fujimoto, Takahiro. 2009. *The Birth of Lean*, p. 54. Cambridge, MA: The Lean Enterprise Institute.
9. Ohno, Taiichi. 1988. *Toyota Production System: Beyond Large-Scale Production*, p. 11. New York, NY: Productivity Press.
10. Shimokawa, Koichi, and Fujimoto, Takahiro. 2009. *The Birth of Lean*, p. 79. Cambridge, MA: The Lean Enterprise Institute.

11. Ohno, Taiichi. 1988. *Toyota Production System: Beyond Large-Scale Production*, p. 69. New York, NY: Productivity Press.

8

The Patois: 8-Step Problem-Solving

Patois is the special language or communication that's common to a particular group.

> Having no problems is the biggest problem of all.[1]

> By asking why five times and answering it each time, we can get to the real root cause of the problem, which is often hidden behind more obvious symptoms …. To tell the truth, the Toyota Production System has been built on the practice and evolution of this scientific approach.[2]

The patois is the dialect of the common people of a region, differing in various respects from the standard language of the rest of the country. The language of the Toyota Template differs from the language spoken by today's typical "lean" initiatives. This patois is a defining characteristic.

After an introduction to the mindset of the culture, the logical next item is learning to speak the language. This language is critical to a lean culture. The language of the Toyota Template is 8-Step problem-solving. At Toyota, this is expressed using the A3. Problems are addressed in this language, whether a formal A3 is done or not. What this means is that the thinking pattern of the 8-Step process is followed for all problems. Over time at Toyota, I learned to view problems in this way, because this is how problems are communicated. When a problem arose, this sequence automatically came to mind. What is the problem? What is the current condition? What's the goal? Root cause? Countermeasures? How to implement? Follow-up?

Communication among the various departments and groups used this language as well. This is a very important point, because it standardized and required everyone, at every level, to look at problems through the same lens. It greatly reduced opinions. This thinking sequence became our language. This is critical to the success of a lean company in the long term, because you're developing a problem-solving culture. I cannot stress this point enough.

As I said, Toyota's 8-Step problem-solving method is the "language of the Toyota Template." This ability to solve problems is what differentiates Toyota from everyone else. In my experience, this is a key missing ingredient in many lean efforts today. As Ohno said, the Toyota Production System (TPS) was built on this scientific approach. So, why is it uncommon in lean implementations? I don't have an answer, but I've often wondered why there's little focus on teaching people how to solve problems. Maybe problem-solving is not practiced because of the emphasis on tools. Solutions to problems seem to be some tool. This illustrates one of the pitfalls in problem-solving. Jumping to a countermeasure without doing the analysis is easy to do, especially when very familiar with the process. However, when the process is followed, there's usually much that's not known about the problem. What I've realized is that when real problem-solving is practiced, the best countermeasures will be found and implemented. As critical as this language is to Toyota, it's very disappointing to see it rarely used. It's important to be reminded that Ohno said that TPS is built on the practice and evolution of this scientific approach.[3] Let that sink in. *The TPS is built on this scientific approach to problem-solving.*

During my initial training at the Tsutsumi plant in Toyota City, the question was raised regularly by my trainer, "Do you have an idea to do this better?" This plant had been open since 1964. What could a young man who'd never seen the inside of an automobile plant possibly offer that would be an improvement? The constant emphasis on what I thought required me to give it a try. As a young American, I was thinking a profound, meaningful change, though I had no idea what that might be. My trainer steered me into the weeds. He wanted me to think about small improvements. So, when I came up with a few ideas, my trainer made a much bigger deal of my small contributions than I felt they deserved. He was encouraging.

My training was as a Team Leader in the Body Weld conveyance group. Our group was responsible for delivering 100% of the parts to the line that were used to build the Camry and handling all kanbans that pertained to these deliveries. Most of my training in Japan centered around two processes. The first was delivering boxed parts from outside vendors to the production lines on a timed route. I was put on a tow motor and led by my trainer on his bike to a covered area just outside the Body Weld Dept.

Here, trucks came in from suppliers with boxes stacked neatly on wooden pallets. A team member unloaded these stacks with a forklift directly onto the dollies. I'd hitch up to a string of dollies and proceed through the area, delivering parts to the line. When finished, I'd pull my dollies back to the covered area and hitch up to a new set of loaded dollies. After running the route a few times, it dawned on me that the boxes were loaded on the pallets from the outside supplier in the delivery order of the route. This was my first impression of "what was needed, when it was needed, in the amount needed." The Body Weld supplier, an outside vendor, had loaded the boxes in the precise sequence that the route ran through the plant. Interesting concept.

The second process I learned during my training was to ride a bicycle on a timed route to pick up kanban cards from drop boxes at the processes. I had a basket on my bike that I used to store my take as I meandered through the plant. When I was finished, there were prescribed places to deliver the kanbans. The first helpful thing I noticed was that all the kanban boxes were painted red. This "visual" made the route running easier, because the red color was easy to see. Also, they were mostly located in the same location on the flow racks. This narrowed my sight and made the job more efficient. Visual controls … another interesting concept.

While repeating these tasks daily, I finally came up with a few ideas. My first suggestion was to turn the location signage at each flow rack perpendicular to the production lines instead of parallel. As I drove my routes, the locations were difficult to see, because they weren't facing me. Turning them perpendicular made the locations easy to see. My second suggestion required a little more thought.

Part of the protective equipment required in the Body Shop was to wear Kevlar gloves with cotton gloves over them. Grasping became a little more difficult, especially the kanban cards. When the cards were laid flat in the small red boxes, they were a little difficult to grasp and pick up. I suggested placing a short length of small rubber hose in each box to prop up the kanbans and prevent them from lying flat in the boxes. For me, this made them easier to pick up. My trainer quickly had both suggestions implemented.

Something else that I became aware of after the fact was that I was going to be paid for my little suggestions. My trainer showed me how to fill out the suggestion form. I still have the original form I completed for the hose idea, complete with a drawing by my trainer. For this input, I was paid 500 yen! (About $4 in 1988. To give some perspective, my starting wage was a little over $10/h.) Not only did Toyota want to know what my ideas might be, but they were going to pay me extra for them too!

Figure 8.1 shows the original suggestion form for my rubber hose idea from my Japan training at the Tsutsumi plant.

One afternoon, near the end of my training time at the Tsutsumi plant, I was met at the conclusion of the boxed parts route by a person I'd not met or even seen previously. He had on a dark suit, a white shirt, and a tie. He bowed and introduced himself, and I did likewise. His translator said he

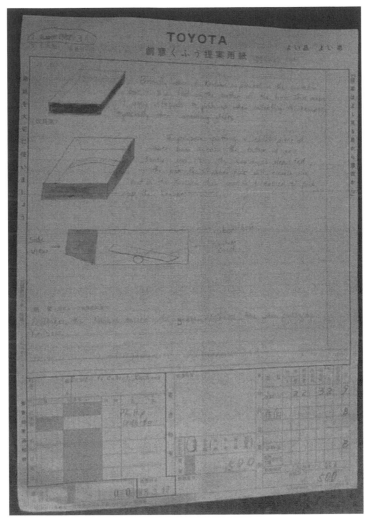

FIGURE 8.1
Original suggestion for Hose Kaizen from training at the Tsutsumi plant (March, 1988).

wanted to know about my improvement ideas. After I explained what I'd suggested, he thanked me, bowed again, and was on his way. I don't recall his name or his role, but I can tell you he was the only person I'd seen in the Body Shop wearing a suit and tie! My thought was that it was an interesting meeting, but I hadn't yet put it together.

Less than a year after my Japan training, I was promoted to Group Leader. I was to lead the second shift conveyance group, which was launching in April, 1989. Sometime after I went to second shift, I was requested to take a course at the Training Center called "Kaizen Train-the-Trainer." This course taught me how to lead a kaizen using the Toyota problem-solving process. After completing the course requirements, I was quickly leading week-long kaizens with other group leaders. Honestly, I didn't know much more than my cohorts. But I found it interesting and fun.

What I didn't realize at the time was that I'd been given the language of the Toyota culture ... 8-Step problem-solving using the A3. (It was called 7-step at this time.) This problem-solving method changed my world view. I began to see every problem in this way, as did everyone else! I began to describe problems with facts and personal observation. I learned how to investigate potential causes. When I left notes for the other shift (we playfully referred to the other shift as the "other we's"), I left them in this format. I even applied this thinking in my personal life.

Moving from a condo into a house with a large yard required me to mow every week in the summer. During one of my mowings, I ran out of gas. I went to get my gas can to fill up my tank and discovered it was empty too. I had to get in my car and make a trip to the station to fill my gas can. As I was mowing later, I thought about having to stop in the middle and making a trip to the gas station. It had prolonged my mowing time (I overcycled!). So, I came up with a countermeasure. I bought a second gas can. When I emptied the first can, it was my signal to get more gas. The second can allowed me to continue mowing without making an immediate trip to the station. This additional work-in-process unit of gas allowed me to get gas at my convenience. This eliminated my problem. Later, when I purchased a gas-powered weed eater, I bought one that used the same gas/oil mixture as my mower so that I didn't need two types of fuel. These are simple examples of how this thinking affected my world view. Let's briefly go over the 8-Step problem-solving using the A3.

The theme, or title, goes at the top left of the A3. This is what you're talking about. For example, on-time-delivery (OTD) in shipping. This is easy and should take no time.

The first step in the problem-solving process is to develop a good problem statement. The problem statement defines the scope. It narrows the focus so that it's clear what is being addressed. Arriving at a concise problem statement employs current observations and facts.

A problem is one of the following:

1. Deviation from the standard. For example, if our standard is 80% OTD, but we don't achieve it, then we have a problem.
2. The standard is met, but a higher standard is now required/desired. In this case, we consistently achieve 80% OTD, but we want/need to reach a higher goal, say 90%.
3. Performance to a standard is not consistently achieved. Here, we sometimes get our 80%, but many times we don't.
4. No standard exists.

Here's an easy way to make a good problem statement. Form the problem statement from the answers to the following questions:

- Who does it affect? Customers
- What does it affect? Revenuc
- How much is the effect? Average OTD is 61% over the last 3 months
- Where is it a problem? Shipping
- When is it a problem? Daily

Write these questions down and answer each one. Make a concise statement from the answers. For example, "Daily OTD at shipping has averaged 61% over the last 3 months, negatively affecting customers and revenue." Again, it's critical to arrive at a good problem statement that answers these questions, because it focuses the problem-solving efforts.

The second step in the process is to paint a true picture of the current condition. This involves a heavy dose of observation, beginning at the workplace, in relation to your problem statement. Avoid preconceived notions or countermeasures during the investigation. This is sometimes difficult, especially if very familiar with the process. However, preconceived notions about countermeasures will torpedo the problem-solving efforts.

Many times, we think we know what's going on, or what should be happening, but it's not the reality at the worksite. You must get all the relevant facts. Talk to the folks doing the work. Watch what they do. This should prompt a lot of "why" questions. Go upstream to see how the product or information is processed and handed off. Take lots of notes, even if unsure of the relevance of the information. There is plenty to understand about the process that is not easily seen through casual observation.

In my view, the number one reason for the failure of a kaizen is the lack of a deep understanding of the current condition. If we don't have a firm grasp of what's really happening, we can be led to implement countermeasures that do not address the problem. Improvement can be made anywhere efforts are focused to truly understand the current condition. This is critically important in problem-solving.

The third step in the problem-solving process is to formulate a S.M.A.R.T. goal statement. Many know the acronym, but for those who are unfamiliar, I'll briefly explain.

S = The goal should be *Specific.*
M = It should be *Measurable.*
A = It should be *Achievable.*
R = It should be *Realistic.*
T = It should be *Time-Targeted.*

An easy way I've found to make a goal statement is to think this way: *Do what, to what, by when.*

For example, increase OTD to 80% by 12/6. We then need to step back and determine whether the goal meets the criteria. Is it specific, measurable, achievable, realistic, and time-targeted? One word of caution here. Sometimes the goal is achievable but not realistic. For example, if the goal can be achieved but requires excessive expense, excessive time, or unavailable resources, then it may not be realistic.

After developing a concise, focused problem statement, an accurate and full understanding of the current condition, and a S.M.A.R.T. goal, we next tackle the root cause. Many times, there are several factors in the cause. In other words, many times, there is no one root cause. This is more typical with larger problems, such as our OTD example. This problem could be related to several different factors, such as disorganization at shipping, staffing, lack of heijunka and pull upstream causing timing issues, quality issues, and so on. So, sometimes, instead of going through the 5-Why exercise, the root cause is "several contributing factors," because it's true.

However, with problems where there appears to be one root cause, the 5-Why exercise is important. This is often applicable with quality problems. It can also be a hard and frustrating thing to do. Even Ohno said, "it is difficult to do even though it sounds easy."[4]

After completing the 5-Why exercise, don't forget to confirm you have the actual root cause. This is done using the "therefore test." Begin by repeating the last answer, followed by "therefore," then the next answer going backward. If it makes sense using the "therefore test," then you've got a well-reasoned root cause. This check will highlight flaws in the reasoning (Figure 8.2).

At this point, we know the current condition and the goal, so the question is what, specifically, should be done to move us from where we are now to where we want to be. In other words, what needs to be done to get to the goal? The next step is to brainstorm countermeasures that address each contributing factor (or the root cause). This is easier and more obvious if a good job has been done on the current condition and the cause analysis. Some of the proposed countermeasures should be tested if possible and if it makes sense. By implementing countermeasures that apply to corresponding problems from the current condition, improvements are made more rapidly. As Ohno said, "For every problem, we must have a specific countermeasure."[5]

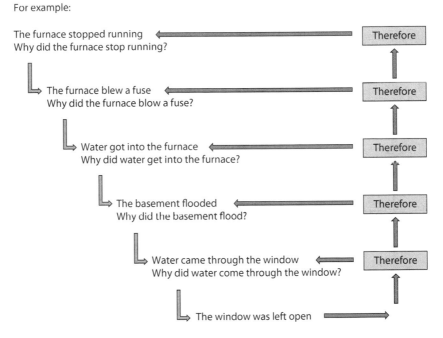

FIGURE 8.2
Example of 5-Why using the "therefore test" to check validity.

After determining the countermeasures, copy them into the implementation plan. The implementation plan assigns order, responsibility, and timing to each countermeasure. After putting them into the plan, we must determine the order of implementation. Sometimes, we may want to try one countermeasure and leave everything else "as is" for a control. Other times, we want to implement several of the countermeasures. In this case, we should consider the order of events, because sometimes the order matters. Responsibility belongs to everyone ultimately, but assigning responsibility and a completion date ensures that someone specific is leading each activity, there are expectations, and the plan is visual for everyone.

A caution on implementation. Every effort should be made to mitigate any negative effect of the countermeasure implementation on production. To do this, we must anticipate what could possibly go wrong. Ask some "what if" questions. And if the countermeasures have a negative effect on production, we must anticipate how to unwind what's been done to restore the original condition. Don't be afraid to try out the countermeasures, but anticipate what failure might look like, and be ready to react.

After the countermeasures are implemented, we measure the results. This is called the *follow-up*. The follow-up should be a restatement of the goal statement. Was the goal achieved by the assigned date? If our goal was to increase OTD to 80% by a certain date (from 61%) but we only get to 73%, have we failed? Absolutely not! We've increased significantly (almost 20%). However, we're not yet where we want to be (80%). Now what?

Problem-solving is an iterative process. Start over with the problem-solving from the new current condition. Undoubtedly, some things have changed. The new current condition is not the same as the original condition. Because the current condition has changed, we must observe again and determine what the new current condition looks like now. It's quite possible that we see other issues that were not visible before. What do the operators have to say now? It could be that we've exposed the real cause. Maybe this time we zero in on the specific root cause? For example, it could be that the lack of pulling orders and heijunka are the big issues now. Lots of products are being made, but the timing is off. We may realize that production isn't "synced up," as Ohno said.

As changes are made, they must be standardized. This will help you hold on to the gains that have been made. Of course, this is done through standard work. Additionally, after making changes in the process, training may be involved.

The Toyota 8-Step problem-solving method has been used successfully for decades at Toyota. It's an iterative, logical, rational process to solve problems in all aspects of a business. The Toyota 8-Step problem-solving method is the "language of the Toyota Template." This is an indispensable condition for a lean culture. Let me give one more example that really illustrated to me, personally, the importance of the emphasis on problem-solving and the major influence on the culture.

At Toyota, we had a suggestion system. Team members and team leaders were encouraged to make suggestions to improve their processes by completing a one-page form, which mirrored 8-Step problem-solving. It was voluntary, but many people participated because of the reward. Toyota paid for these suggestions. The minimum pay-out for a simple suggestion was $10. If the idea had any effect on safety, it was worth $3 more. Many suggestions paid $13. And this was paid for *each* suggestion.

For example, if someone had the idea to paint a stop sign on the floor at an intersection, then they were paid $13 after implementation. But if they implemented the same idea at 10 intersections, then the pay-out was $130! Additionally, the team member was paid for their time to implement their idea. Sometimes, this meant working overtime. This was a very nice incentive for team members to become involved in problem-solving and continuous improvement activities.

To me, it seemed like the company was just giving money away. Virtually any suggestions, especially obvious and easy ones, were encouraged. I had a conveyance group at the time, and some of my members carried small pads of paper with them and made notes on anything they saw that could be improved. Because they traveled all over the Body Weld department, they saw many areas. As a result, some members would sit in the break room at lunch and write out suggestions on the form and submit them to me. Many times, I was flooded with suggestion forms to check on for approval. Sometimes, I felt guilty about approving suggestions, because it seemed too easy.

But I was wrong. Even though sometimes an idea was implemented in several places, and it seemed so easy, I missed the genius behind the process. By making the process lenient, at least in the first few years, the momentum that was created was incredible. Many team members got involved, even folks who might not normally have been interested. While Toyota later tightened up the criteria (later, one idea that was implemented in multiple locations was paid one time), the fire had been fueled.

Many, many team members had been involved. They'd experienced the willingness of Toyota to listen to their ideas and allow, even encourage and expect, them to improve their process. In my experience, team members were more than willing to make suggestions for improvement, because they understood that Toyota was serious about kaizen and valued their input. After all, the team members are the experts on their respective processes. They see things during their work that aren't apparent to the leader. These problems would never be addressed if they weren't encouraged and expected to speak up.

Another aspect of problem-solving in TPS is the Quality Circle (QC). QCs were formed, voluntarily, in many groups. The QC leader was required to take a class to understand how to lead and facilitate the QC. Their report-out tool was the A3. I had several in my groups over the years. As the Group Leader, I was the QC advisor. My role was to assist from the outside: provide general guidance, give them time to meet or work on their problem, and assist with any barriers or resources needed.

During the time that I had the conveyance group, one of my Team Leaders started a QC to address a safety issue related to parts that were shipped over from Japan. At the time, we received "modules" from Japan. These were large boxes of parts, approximately 4′ × 8′, that contained 12–16 part #s in each module with 40 of each part. The module was loaded onto a dolly that was pulled by a tugger on a route. The parts were unloaded at stops along the route, 40 at a time. The QC decided to address a safety issue with the way the parts were placed in the modules, affecting everyone in the group.

They repacked each module and ran them in the new way. There were suggestions and buy-in from both shifts. In doing this, they realized that when they repacked them, they'd created more room in the modules. This led them to increase several module quantities to 45 of each part. When this was done, they realized something else. There would be tremendous savings in shipping costs, because Japan was shipping more parts in each module. The savings came to about $1.2 million per year. They did a great job! The teamwork was excellent, and implementation costs were very low. They basically just changed the way the modules were packed using the same resources. The interesting point here is that what started as an effort to make the delivery of modules safer not only achieved that goal but also resulted in large savings.

Concerning problem-solving, a strong indicator to determine whether a company is serious about a lean culture is how they view and handle problems. Are they highlighted as opportunities for improvement, or are they hidden?

The Patois: The language of the Toyota Template is 8-Step problem-solving.

Culture: A common language is a defining characteristic of a culture. Consistent, repetitive use of the language created the problem-solving culture. Employee participation is an integral component in problem-solving. Focus is on the problem, not the person. Speaking the same language is very important in any culture. The patois is one of the most critical contributors to a lean culture.

ENDNOTES

1. Ohno, Taiichi. 2006. Toyota-Global.com. Released March, www.toyota-global.com/company/toyota_traditions/quality/mar_apr_2006.html.
2. Ohno, Taiichi. 1988. *Toyota Production System: Beyond Large-Scale Production*, p. 17. New York, NY: Productivity Press.
3. Ohno, Taiichi. 1988. *Toyota Production System: Beyond Large-Scale Production*, p. 17. New York, NY: Productivity Press.
4. Ibid.
5. Ibid., p. 114.

9

The Pattern: Flow, Pull, and Heijunka

A pattern is a dependable set of attributes that are prevalent in a particular group or company.

> Many good companies have respect for individuals, and practice kaizen and other TPS tools. ... But what is important is having all the elements together as a system. It must be practiced every day in a very consistent manner, not in spurts.[1]

Ohno and others spent a tremendous amount of time on these three subjects. Ohno talks extensively about these elements in all three of his books, referencing just-in-time (JIT), kanban, supermarkets, continuous flow, pull, leveling, and using various other terms. These concepts have received considerable coverage by those who were involved in the evolution of the Toyota Production System (TPS). However, in my experience, these critical concepts are not viewed with the same importance as Ohno and others viewed them. Ohno said, "The first step in implementing Toyota-style production is to create flow; next is to establish JIT production."[2] In Ohno's development of TPS, flow came early, the first thing he did in the machine shop. Next came pull, after he'd observed American supermarkets. Heijunka was instituted after pulling.

In view of the Toyota Template, the pattern consists of the "critical must conditions." Flow, pull, and heijunka are the concepts that are required for a JIT production system. Remember, Ohno was building a system based on the elimination of waste. Everything he did was focused on this goal. Flow, pull, and heijunka were done in his continuous efforts to banish waste. Some of the tools that were implemented along the way, such as standard work or 5S, can be used outside of a JIT system. This is the case in many tool approaches, because this "pattern" is ignored. Standard work, problem-solving, kanban, and so on can be implemented without flow, pull, and heijunka, but the effect on production is greatly diminished and difficult to sustain. These three are closely related, dependent on each other, and are critical "musts" for the success of a lean initiative.

CONTINUOUS FLOW: ALIGNMENT OF PROCESSES IN THE ORDER OF VALUE ADDED

[I]n the plant we must first rearrange the equipment in the order that people work and in the order that value is added to create a flow. In creating flow, it is not enough to look at just part of the process.[3]

[A]rranging processes in the natural workflow was a precondition for linking the processes and lines as a pull system.[4]

To put this in context, Ohno started to arrange equipment in this manner in the machine shop in the late 1940s to eliminate waste. By 1953, "stores" had been set up at the various stages of the manufacturing processes. This was the beginning of an effort to realize Kiichiro Toyoda's idea that "it is best to have the various parts arrive alongside the assembly line just-in-time."[5]

There are many advantages realized when continuous flow is created. The most important one, cited by Ohno, is that creating flow is a "precondition for linking the processes and lines as a pull system."[6] This is the origin of one-piece flow. Linking processes to one another in order makes it possible to implement a pull system. It's a "precondition."

One advantage of flow is the ability to combine work or move work around between processes as needed. When they're connected in order, it's much easier to see and understand where imbalances exist. When processes are not connected in continuous flow, these imbalances are more difficult to understand. There tends to be much unnecessary batch building and transporting of parts between processes. Additionally, it's more difficult to differentiate between the normal and the abnormal.

The improvement of what Ohno called the "baton passing zone" is also possible. This is the area between processes where work handoff occurs. Ohno equated production to a relay race where "a faster runner can make up for a slower runner in the baton passing zone."[7]

When processes are arranged in the order in which value is added to the product, connected processes can aid one another in times of need. For example, if the upstream process experiences a delay due to a scrap part, the downstream process can assist by moving over to help in catching up. There's no telling how many times this happens in a day at Toyota. Likely thousands of times throughout the plant. Additionally, team leaders will step in on many occasions to assist team members when they experience a problem. "To improve the efficiency of the line, the supervisor must establish a baton passing zone where workers have a chance to catch up."[8]

A third big advantage is the potential to minimize, or even eliminate, the need to transport parts between processes. When they're not aligned in the order in which value is added, parts from upstream must be transported to the downstream process. This requires additional people and equipment. When they're aligned, transporting can be avoided by simply passing along the product with rollers or a conveyor, particularly in a one-piece flow situation. In fact, in one-piece flow areas, this is the norm.

Finally, inventory can be greatly reduced. One of the primary reasons for buffers between processes is the distance between them. When processes are not well connected, more buffer is required. If excessive buffers, or work-in-process (WIP), are required due to poor process connections, then money is tied up on the floor in inventory unnecessarily. Cash flow is negatively affected. It's possible to have millions of dollars sitting on the production floor between processes in work-in-process (WIP) when it could be avoided.

Continuous flow is most important in processes where items are, or can be, made one at a time. Identifying these processes and closely linking them together in order should be done first. The opportunity to eliminate waste in the form of excess inventory and transportation by simply establishing continuous flow is the result. And more importantly, as Ohno said, flow is a precondition for implementation of a pull system.

> Culture: Creating continuous flow is another contributor to the building of the lean culture. It requires multi-skilled workers, reducing boredom and improving teamwork in the baton passing zone. When employees are dependent on one another and help each other, information, communication, and the general working conditions are improved. It's also critical to the property of waste elimination.

PULL: PACES AND PRIORITIZES PRODUCTION, AND PROMOTES PROBLEM-SOLVING

> Looking at things individually they say they are doing a good job of producing gears, or that they are using robots very well, or that they can do the work with just 3 people. But these items can only be sold when they are together as a set.[9]

> [O]nly considering the production plan for each process, we would produce parts without regard to the later processes. Waste would result – defective parts on the one hand, huge inventories of parts not needed immediately on the other. This reduces both productivity and profitability. Even worse, there would be no distinction between normal and abnormal states on each assembly line.[10]

> The Toyota Production System is a pull method. To understand its tremendous success, one has to grasp the philosophy behind it without being sidetracked by particular aspects of the system, such as Kanban.[11]

> It takes great effort to practice the 6 rules of kanban ... thus a half-hearted introduction of a pull system brings a hundred harms and not a single gain.[12]

I've often heard people say that the processes must be stabilized before a pull system can be introduced into production. What this means exactly is not clear. Generally, having standard work, inventory accuracy, and 5S are mentioned. All desirable conditions, for sure. No doubt, having stability on the manufacturing floor is a condition required to achieve efficiency.

Stabilizing production consists of two very important concepts. They are pull production and heijunka, or level loading. Along with flow, these were the concepts that changed the game for Toyota. If there is a silver bullet to TPS, continuous flow, pull, and heijunka are the three conditions that must be met.

> An old-timer in the assembly section told me how President Kiichiro Toyota said to him that the most efficient way to assemble parts in an assembly plant was when each part arrived Just in Time.[13]

At Toyota, the decision to pull production through the plant was the beginning of Kiichiro Toyoda's idea that parts arrive at the workplace in the quantity and at the time needed. This requires a well-thought-out plan. Pulling is a major change if pushing with schedules has been the practice. In the beginning, the actual orders must be pulled through the plant. The pulling of individual parts is a result of the pulling of the orders. On more than one occasion, I've heard this idea of pulling interpreted as simply setting up parts on a kanban. Some call it a "supermarket strategy." Setting up parts on a kanban is a good idea *only if* the orders are being pulled through the plant with heijunka. The fact is that the kanban does not work well unless the orders or jobs are pulled. When a kanban system is set up for a group of parts in a push system, other problems will ensue. Pulling begins at the end of the plant, in shipping, and moves upstream. Pulling must be the method of making things in lean manufacturing. Ohno said, "Kanban must work effectively to maintain just-in-time in the plant. And for Kanban to be effective, stabilization and production leveling are indispensable conditions."[14] This is a very important point. *Heijunka and pull are indispensable conditions.*

In a push system, such as Material Resource Planning (MRP), orders are pushed to the various areas of the floor based on a schedule over a given period. From an efficiency standpoint, there are two problems with MRP systems. One is timing. Products, or sub-assemblies, related to the same order are manufactured at various rates in the departments where they're made. Each area works in the silo of its own schedule. Their focus is to meet their schedule. Typically, the problem is not that each area can't make the items on its schedule. The problem is timing, or synchronization.

One timing issue is that the process receiving the orders doesn't work toward the needs of its customers. In an effort to maximize their work in an efficient manner, they work at their own pace and in their own order, irrespective of customer needs. No attachment to the customer exists. This order may be determined simply by the fact that the easiest items are made first. Or maybe, the material needed for a particular item happens to be available. No matter what the reason, each department is attempting to maximize its own productivity without regard to the effect on its customer.

In batch build processes, parts should be batched to maximize process efficiency. In a push system, the batch quantities change with every order. Since the batch quantity is linked to the projected demand over time for a particular item, this projected demand, and thus the batch quantity, can be highly variable. Therefore, the batch quantity will always be a suboptimal number. Furthermore, because the exact quantities are made based on the order, when a quality problem arises anywhere in the process, a shortage will occur.

For example, the processes must batch by part number to minimize changeover of equipment or material. In this case, the entire time period's worth, say 1 week's worth, of Part A is built, then Part B, and so on. By the end of Monday, the process has built all the week's requirements for A and B. The problem is that on Monday, their internal customer has 10 orders requiring parts A, B, C, D, and E. The internal customer will receive parts C, D, and E later than required, which prevents them from building the 10 orders. Timing!

Additionally, the customer must store a week's worth of parts A and B that they received on Monday in their area. Too early is the same as too much. And remember, too much, or overproduction, is the worst type of waste. They may also have begun to build their 10 orders, only to find out later that they won't have all the parts needed to complete their orders on Monday. Now, they must store partially built orders until parts C, D, and E arrive the next day. This results in lots of excess WIP, excessive handling, and storage problems. In addition, and maybe less obviously, this type of production is disrespectful and frustrating to employees who come to work to do a good job.

A second timing problem is that the upstream process and its downstream customers are not synced up—the same issue that confronted Toyota years ago. Synchronization cannot be scheduled. In a push system, because processes don't run at the same pace, there is no connection between them. Each is working off its own schedule. Either the upstream process is too slow, causing wait time, or the upstream process buries its customer with more parts than they can use. And rarely the right ones. When this happens, it can become difficult to find what's needed, even though lots of parts are present. The opposite can also be true. The downstream process can be slower or faster than its upstream supplier. How can the actual state of the current condition be determined? Ohno said:

> [O]nly considering the production plan for each process, we would produce parts without regard to the later processes. Waste would result – defective parts on the one hand, huge inventories of parts not needed immediately on the other. This reduces both productivity and profitability. Even worse, there would be no distinction between normal and abnormal states on each assembly line.[15]

There is some good news. You don't have to throw out your MRP system. Just because the system makes the schedule doesn't mean all the schedules must go to production en masse. Use the MRP system to make the schedule, and then, separately, pull the orders in the needed sequence through the plant. Toyota has a schedule, but it's pulled through the plant.

Additionally, timing issues can often lead to capacity questions. Sometimes, when items are not at the right place, at the right time, in the right quantity, the knee jerk assumption is that it's because there is a lack of capacity. Acting on this assumption could lead to additional expense such as overtime, adding labor, or even the purchase of additional equipment. The poor timing root cause is difficult to countermeasure when pushing using schedules and can lead to poor decisions.

Pulling is the countermeasure. It's the only way to sync up products throughout production. A JIT system requires that components mate up as they move down the production line. When beginning to pull, there will likely be a delay at the point at which parts should come together. When this happens, a bottleneck exists. This problem is addressed like any other. It's time to do some problem-solving! What caused the delay, and what needs to be done to countermeasure the problem?

This is a good time to talk about TAKT time. TAKT time is the time that should be taken to produce something. It's based on customer demand. TAKT may differ in different parts of the plant and/or with different products. Daily total operating time is determined based on machinery operating at 100% efficiency during regular working hours: in other words, what could be made if the line ran at 100%.

On a multi-model production line, TAKT time allows parts of different types to be produced. TAKT time also allows the right parts to arrive at the right process at the right time. TAKT time is the rate at which each product should be made. TAKT time is a calculation that can change over time.

$$\text{TAKT time} = \frac{\text{Straight time work time in seconds}}{\text{Required production \#}}$$

Another important aspect of pulling through the plant is the use of predetermined buffers. No buffers would obviously be the ideal, but the reality is that there are several good reasons to have buffers within and between processes and departments. At Toyota, we had many buffers for smoothing product flow.

One reason for a buffer is that it mitigates downtime between departments. This is especially true between areas with a lot of automated equipment. Equipment will fail from time to time. That's just a fact. Having a buffer between these areas and the downstream customer to cover these times when downtime occurs makes good sense. Otherwise, this machine downtime could shut down an entire area. In fact, if there were no buffer between areas with lots of automation, every time a machine stopped in one area, this could result in stopping production in its customer's area. To be clear, I'm not advocating large buffers because machines don't run well. This is about normal expected production loss due to delays caused by machine problems.

Another reason could be the distance between supplier and customer. When customers and their suppliers cannot be closely located, then some buffer is needed between them due to the distance. This could be between two processes on a line or between two processes that are clearly separated. An example might be the distance between areas, departments, or lines.

A third reason for a buffer could be for heijunka. Every department may have different requirements for smoothing production. There could be a need to rearrange products for the downstream department's heijunka requirements. If the next department needs some buffer to rearrange the incoming products in a way that provides for smoother flow through their area, then a buffer is needed for this activity. More about this one later.

And, of course, building in batches is another obvious situation where buffers are required. Some products in production are pulled one at a time, or one-piece flow, through the plant. But many parts must be built, and subsequently pulled, in batches. This situation exists with a machine that makes large quantities of multiple part numbers. A stamping press is a good example. A press can make many parts quickly, but the dies/material must be changed out when a different part number is made. Making one piece at a time makes no sense here. A press may make 40 different part numbers for an auto. The questions for the press operator are which part number should be made, when should it be made, and how many should be made? (Right part, right quantity, right time.) In push systems, a schedule is used to make this determination, and we've covered the timing and other problems with schedules.

> In 1956, I toured U.S. production plants at General Motors, Ford, and other machinery companies. But my strongest impression was the extent of the supermarkets prevalence in America …. we made a connection between supermarkets and the just-in-time system …. From the supermarket we got the idea of viewing the earlier process in a production line as a kind of store.[16]

Supermarkets use a pull system, and for good reason. The obvious issue that requires supermarkets to use a pull system is spoilage. Food wholesalers earn 3%–4% earnings before interest, taxes, depreciation and amortization (EBITDA)/sales versus a general industrial average EBITDA/sales across all sectors of the economy of >15%.[17] Grocers must be much more conscious of waste than other industries, because they have less margin for error. Many food items cannot be held for very long in inventory, because they go bad. Were they to use a push system whereby they bought fresh produce or meat according to a schedule, their spoilage would increase dramatically, and they probably wouldn't be in business long.

So, as Ohno observed, the modern American grocery stores use a pull method. By using a pull system in the grocery business, they can easily and quickly see their waste. Visibility is a major advantage to a pull system. Similarly, manufacturers who use pull can also identify wastes much more easily and quickly. In a push method in manufacturing, the waste is not as obvious as wilted lettuce and thus, a little more difficult to see.

The condition of the Toyota Template is to level pull the actual orders so that they arrive at their respective destinations along the way and at the customer when they are needed. Manufacturers make many parts, or sub-assemblies, that must sync up to move to an internal customer or to be sold to an external customer. If making cabinets, the doors, sides, tops, and bottoms must show up together at the assembly line for the cabinet to be assembled. This applies to most businesses. Even in businesses where many sub-assemblies are shipped to a worksite for assembly onsite, all parts must arrive in time for assembly to take place. Many times, in these circumstances, the manufacturer is unable to ship partial deliveries to a worksite, because the customer must assemble the product in the field. It can be costly to receive bits and pieces of the total product randomly because of a synchronization problem in manufacturing. Customers also don't want to pay for a partial product in these circumstances, and they shouldn't.

A substantial benefit gained when changing from a push to a pull system is the large reduction in inventory on the floor, or WIP. This is because the buffers between and within processes are now controlled. Each buffer has a predetermined quantity, and if a buffer is full, production upstream stops. Overproduction, in terms of WIP, is eliminated. What was once unsynchronized production in the push system becomes synchronized in the pull system. This reduction in WIP can be large, likely 50% or more. This means that money previously tied up in inventory is now cash in the bank.

The reduction of WIP in manufacturing is also beneficial to lead times. Little's Law says that

$$\text{Lead time} = \text{WIP units} / \text{units per time period}$$

If WIP is 100 units and you can process 25 units/day, then $100/25 = 4$-day lead time. Now, let's say that after implementing a pull system, the WIP is reduced to 50 units. Now, $50/25 = 2$-day lead time.

When WIP is reduced, lead time decreases.

> As for timing…You could only get the timing right if you conveyed the parts by having the following process pick them up. You'd screw up the timing if you simply pushed the parts onto the following process according to a production plan.[18]

Pull production is the only way to get the timing right!

Predetermined buffers provide another significant benefit to pull: the ability to see and understand the abnormal condition. Buffers are a visual control. It's very easy to determine whether the supplier is behind by observing the buffer. Conversely, if the buffer stays full, then the upstream process must stop, because there's no place to put their product. This may be a signal that there's a problem downstream. This visual control is very useful in understanding where problems occur, aiding in problem-solving.

An additional benefit, which may be less obvious, is headcount reduction. Typically, in a push system, scheduled volumes can fluctuate tremendously from day to day in many processes. One day, this process looks like it can't keep up. The next day, it's another process that appears to be behind. To combat this issue, many processes are staffed to absorb these fluctuations in demand. Over time, processes throughout the plant become overstaffed.

After pull is implemented, production is synchronized, and a pace, dictated by TAKT time, is established. This highlights the staffing situation. Because the pace is steady and established, most processes will be overstaffed. Remember, they were previously staffed to meet the extremes of the daily schedule in each area. Like WIP reduction, this can also result in a very substantial decrease in headcount and labor cost.

Finally, as mentioned previously, when the excess inventory disappears from the floor, good 5S becomes a goal that is much easier to attain.

On JIT, Ohno said, "once decided upon, it should be undertaken with a firm and determined mind."[19]

Culture: Pull systems do away with silo production associated with a push system. This silo mentality is the opposite of teamwork. In a pull environment, there is "tension in the line." Processes are dependent on one another to get their work done. This tension creates a heightened sense of urgency throughout the manufacturing process. It ties internal suppliers and customers together at a pace that requires cooperation and teamwork. The effects of a pull system are very important contributors to a lean culture.

KANBAN: METERING FLOW

The operating method of the Toyota Production System is Kanban.[20]

Kanban is a way to achieve just-in-time; its purpose is just-in-time. Kanban, in essence, becomes the autonomic nerve of the production line.[21]

The Kanban links production in each process to the pace of production in the following process.[22]

I must admit that the first time I encountered a kanban during my training, I was intrigued. My formal introduction to the kanban was during my training on the kanban pick-up route at Tsutsumi. I remember thinking that a kanban was like currency to the processes that used them. They couldn't get more until they presented their "money." One of the first things that aroused my curiosity was all the information on the card and what it meant. My trainer patiently explained each bit and why it was on the card. The information was carefully thought out, considering the information both Toyota and the supplier needed and no more.

It wasn't until later, when I got back to Georgetown, that I became aware of the rules, how to determine the number in circulation, the different types and how they were used, and the importance of time. I also came to understand the reason for only two addresses. The kanban only works as a closed loop. When a third stop is entered into the equation, timing becomes a problem. If a kanban is used internally between two processes, the supplier and the user, it must only circulate between these two locations.

At Toyota, we used two types of kanban, each with a specific purpose. The parts withdrawal kanban was pulled at the user location for reordering another container from the supplier. We always pulled the kanban and dropped it in the kanban post when the first part was used out of the container. This was the rule. This differs from two-bin systems where the container acts as the kanban. In this system, the kanban is effectively dropped after the last part in the container is consumed. Of course, this reduces the lead time and may result in needing an additional container in the system. Also, with the parts withdrawal kanban, the minimum number of kanbans for any part is two. The reason for the two-card minimum is that if one is lost, the process will see that they're running low and can take remedial action. This is something my trainer shared with me. I mention it because I've seen situations where only one parts withdrawal kanban is in circulation. When there's only one kanban, the process may not know the kanban is lost until they're completely out. The second type of kanban is the production instruction, or signal kanban. It's used to signal the upstream producer that it's time to make more. This kanban, which I'll explain later, is used to connect batch production with one-piece flow processes.

> Kanban is a tool for realizing just-in-time. For this tool to work fairly well, the production processes must be managed to flow as much as possible. This is really the basic condition. Other important conditions are leveling production as much as possible and always working in accordance with standard work methods.[23]

A word of caution on the use of the kanban. Though it can be used, the kanban does not work well in a push system. This is because a pull system for a subset of parts has been introduced into a push environment. The effectiveness is minimal at best, and other problems are created in this situation. The timing problem, previously discussed, is amplified when kanban is introduced, because timing is critical in a kanban system. In the long run, this creates distrust of the kanban for replenishment, many times leading to work arounds and collapse. And in the big picture, when a lean tool doesn't work well, there's a tendency to think lean "won't work here."

In the TPS, overproduction is completely prevented by Kanban.[24]

HEIJUNKA: PRODUCTION SMOOTHING

> So, if you're going to make different kinds of assemblies, you need to distribute the production of the different kinds evenly throughout the day …

> If you don't level production, you'll keep running out of parts. You level production by changing the order in which you make things.[25]

> The most important prerequisite of JIT production is production smoothing, or small lot production.[26]

Generally, demand for products is highly variable. Customers don't order the various products you sell in a level fashion. Orders are unpredictable both in volume and in the type of product. This unpredictability can wreak havoc in a manufacturing environment for many reasons. Toyota understood the importance of production smoothing after they began pulling.

> Our biggest problem with this system [pull] was how to avoid throwing the earlier process into confusion when a later process picked up large quantities at a time. Eventually, after trial and error, we came up with production leveling.[27]

Heijunka means level loading or production smoothing over time. In manufacturing, this means level loading of the production floor. There are two aspects. The first, and easier to achieve, is to level load production by volume. The second aspect of heijunka is to level load by product mix or type. This is the more difficult but also yields the greatest benefit.

The lack of production smoothing is a primary and continuous contributor to waste throughout the plant. Mura (unevenness) and muri (overburden) are greatly reduced in *every process* in the plant when heijunka is achieved.

When customers don't order products in an order that leads to level loading of the production process, which is always, the orders arrive at customer service or sales in a random fashion. The question is how to meet customer demand.

One way would be to simply make products in a first-in, first-out (FIFO) sequence in which the orders arrive in customer service. Let's look at a simple example. Let's suppose that you make four different products (A, B, C, and D) that share many of the same processes. Time to produce each varies by product type. A takes 10 minutes, B takes 15 minutes, C requires 20 minutes, and D requires 30 minutes to produce. In this scenario, both mura and muri would be prevalent, because production is at the mercy of chance. Also, each process must be staffed, have materials available, and enough equipment to meet peak production in every process.

An example of heijunka in Body Weld was in the Roof and Cowl area. Customers don't buy the same number of cars with regular roofs as those that have sunroofs. Though it can vary, let's say that one in seven cars sold had sunroofs. The cycle time to build a sunroof is considerably longer than the cycle time for a regular roof. Toyota used a product indicator in the process (a light board to indicate body number and option, in this case which roof) that told the team member which roof to build. In this example, the member would build six roofs, one sunroof, six roofs, one sunroof, and so on. The process layout, machine cycle times, and walk time were set up to enable one person to build both types. After the roofs were built, they went to buffer pallets for each type. A carrier, again responding to body number and type, picked up a roof from the correct pallet, either the sunroof pallet or the regular roof pallet, and delivered it to the Framing Body Line to be mated up with the underbody and side members.

For these sub-assemblies to sync up together on the correct car body, heijunka was established. Production Control arranges them in the build order required to achieve heijunka for Body Weld considering options such as the roof types. Without heijunka, more employees would be required to perform the same work. If the orders were built in a random fashion, the Roof and Cowl area would need to be staffed to handle three or four sunroofs consecutively, since this could happen. In this case, the sunroof members would be very busy, while the regular roof member would be waiting.

Heijunka can be a difficult concept to understand in a traditional manufacturing environment. It's hard for leaders to believe in something when the benefits are less obvious or easy to see. Typically, leaders want to see direct benefits in anything they undertake. How is smoothing production throughout the plant measured? What's the Key Productivity Indicator? There isn't one.

The fascination with tools, the "point kaizen" emphasis, and a lack of problem-solving have led to a focus on symptoms. The lack of production smoothing ensures the introduction of random variation in the form of mura and muri, from the very beginning, into the entire manufacturing system. This variation results in costs that are not easily seen. Delays at various places along the production process result in waiting elsewhere.

The lack of level loading can affect direct costs too. Let's look at an example that illustrates the effect of not level loading.

There was a manufacturer that made items that were boxed up at the end of each assembly line. This was a manual process performed by a worker.

As the items came down the line, the boxer would choose the box based on the size of the product. The company had to stock several different box sizes. There was always some danger of running out of one size or another. The company decided to invest in a corrugated box-making machine that cut boxes to custom sizes. Making boxes the correct size for each product would save some costs.

The plant had two production lines that made the same products. They ran both lines on first shift and neither line on second shift. On third shift, the first line ran for 4 hours; then, the crew would move to the second line and run it for 4 hours. The assembly lines ran:

First shift = 16 hours
Second shift = 0 hours
Third shift = 8 hours
Total = 24 hours

The lines were simple conveyor belts on which the product was loaded and assembled as it moved down the line. Their production volume was maxed out due to environmental reasons. They couldn't make more product.

So, when it was decided to buy corrugated box-making machines—because the lines weren't leveled by volume on each shift—two machines were needed, one for each line. If the 24 hours of production had been spread evenly over three shifts, there would only have been the need for one machine.

In addition to needing two machines instead of one, the assembly area sat empty for an entire shift. Again, if production had been level, half of the assembly area floor space would have been available for another use. Finally, because no production was run on second shift, the buffer from the upstream supplier had to be much larger than needed. This was because the line ran twice as fast on first shift as on third shift. So, the buffer had to be twice what it would have been if production had run evenly on all three shifts.

To achieve heijunka, there are some cases where we must employ the use of buffers. At Toyota, we had buffers in many areas of the plant: between processes, between groups and automated lines within departments, and between departments. One such buffer was critical to heijunka in the largest department in the plant, Assembly.

The Paint Department has a buffer area called the *selectivity bank*. This area held a standard number of cars. It was used to shuffle the cars that came from body into an order that achieved the heijunka requirements for Assembly. This was required because the heijunka requirements for Body Weld were different from the requirements for Assembly. In many manufacturing environments, the requirements from area to area for level loading differ. Buffers can help in heijunka.

"Heijunka is a pre-requisite for Just-in-time delivery."[28] Conversely, JIT delivery is not possible without production smoothing.

> Culture: Heijunka built on this culture by smoothing out production for everyone. This was good for employees, because the work was better paced, and it solved the problems caused by erratic production numbers.

SINGLE-MINUTE EXCHANGE OF DIES (SMED): SET-UP TIME REDUCTION

> In production leveling, batches are made as small as possible in contrast to traditional mass production, where bigger is considered better.[29]

> [W]hile producing item A in quantity, the process may not meet the need for item B. Consequently, shortening setup time and reducing lot sizes becomes necessary.[30]

> Rapid changeovers are an absolute requirement for the Toyota Production System.[31]

One of the challenges to production leveling is the need for batch building processes to make smaller quantities of each part. This is because the downstream processes will no longer be batch building as a result of production smoothing. Many companies are attempting to make things using single-piece flow on assembly lines nowadays. Sub-assemblies are made and passed to the next process one at a time based on some signal. However, as we move upstream to suppliers of the assembly lines, or sub-assemblies feeding the assembly lines, we encounter a problem with one-piece flow. Many of these suppliers, such as stamping presses or injection molders, must make parts in batches or lots.

Some machines or processes must batch, because they make large quantities of multiple part numbers using different materials, tools, and machine settings. Typically, machine operators seek to maximize the use of their machines by building large quantities to reduce the number of changeovers. It wouldn't be practical or make sense for these machines to try to make parts one at a time. A large chunk of production time would be eaten up in changeover time from part to part.

In the auto industry, this is true of the Stamping Department. Stamping presses are very large machines—as large as a 1500 square foot house! A press may make 40–50 different part numbers. In this scenario, one-piece flow is not an option because of the number of different parts and the die change time. This circumstance also exists in industries outside of automobile manufacturing, anywhere batch building must be done. The only way for a press to make all the different part numbers and keep the downstream processes supplied is to build to a store based on actual usage. At Toyota, this is accomplished through use of a Triangle Kanban.

The Triangle Kanban serves the same purpose as the parts withdrawal kanban, except that it's a signal kanban. The kanban is placed on the container of a particular part that represents the trigger point. Before this container is taken to the line in the Body Shop, the kanban is removed and placed on a kanban post in the Stamping area. These kanbans are retrieved by Stamping employees periodically and returned to the press where the parts are to be made. They're generally kept in FIFO order at the press. By this method, all Stamping production is virtually self-scheduled. Of course, there are occasional exceptions, such as scrap. This abnormal situation will accelerate the movement of the particular kanban for that part, so that it is run sooner than normal. In this way, the kanban reacts to the scrap reflexively, in effect, automatically rescheduling the part production sooner.

The Triangle Kanban system accomplishes linkage between batch building and one-piece flow by systematically minimizing batch sizes, which increases changeovers. This is the opposite of what each operator was attempting to do with their individual machines in a push system. The difference is that the Triangle Kanban system considers all parts on each machine that builds in batches in an area. This is a very important point.

The Triangle Kanban moves between the store and the press. This works best when heijunka exists in the plant, because lot sizes and inventories of the various parts can be minimized. This method can be used without heijunka. However, if level loading isn't present, the trigger point of every part in the store must be increased to account for the uneven pull from downstream, and lot sizes will also increase.

Another benefit of this kanban is that only one kanban is needed per part number. This is because the kanban is placed at the trigger point for the part. As I stated previously, when the trigger point is reached, the kanban goes back to the process where the part is produced. No need for a kanban on every container.

Most of us have used a signal kanban before. Think about the reordering of checks. They're used in numerical order. When we arrive at the last 50 or so checks, we have a reorder form. It has all the pertinent information on it: our routing number, account number, address, and so on. The only thing we need to do is select the quantity and drop it off at the bank. This is a signal kanban too.

The Triangle Kanban is the best pull method to move from batch building based on a schedule to batch building based on consumption. This addresses the synchronization problem associated with schedules and batch building.

Figure 9.1 shows a picture of a Triangle Kanban with all the required information needed to make the part.

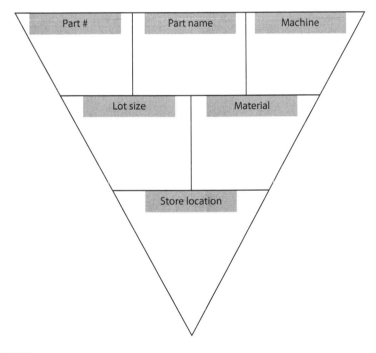

FIGURE 9.1
Example of a Triangle Kanban.

Batch building must be linked with one-piece flow in other industries. There are many plants that have machines that must batch build. Many times, these processes are producing to a schedule. They attempt to somehow match their batch production schedule to their customer's one-piece flow schedule. The process may be able to make all the parts needed, but timing is the problem.

SMED can be done whether you push or pull, because it involves reducing the changeover on one machine at a time. Whether you push or pull, it would be a good thing to do. When implementing a pull system, changeover reduction should be done prior to implementing pull in batch build processes. The ability to changeover quickly and optimize lot sizes is critical in pull systems.

The Pattern: The pattern of the Toyota Template is continuous flow, pull production, and heijunka.

Culture: Continuous flow, pull production, and heijunka are critical concepts in building a lean culture. Continuous flow requires the need for multi-skilled employees. This makes the work safer and more interesting for the employees. Pull production to TAKT creates tension in the line, which in turn, increases the sense of urgency in production processes. This sets a consistent work pace for the employees. Heijunka addresses unevenness and overburden by providing a steady and smooth work environment, which is respectful of employees and physically and mentally beneficial. All three contribute to the lean culture by showing respect for the employees.

ENDNOTES

1. Liker, Jeffrey K. 2004. *The Toyota Way: 14 Management Principles from the World's Greatest Manufacturer*, p. 27. New York, NY: McGraw-Hill.
2. Ohno, Taiichi. 1988. *Just-In-Time for Today and Tomorrow*, p. 18. Cambridge, MA: Productivity Press.
3. Ibid., p. 17.
4. Shimokawa, Koichi and Fujimoto, Takahiro. 2009. *The Birth of Lean*, p. 79. Cambridge, MA: The Lean Enterprise Institute.
5. Ohno, Taiichi. 1988. *Just-In-Time for Today and Tomorrow*, p. 9. Cambridge, MA: Productivity Press.
6. Shimokawa, Koichi and Fujimoto, Takahiro. 2009. *The Birth of Lean*, p. 79. Cambridge, MA: The Lean Enterprise Institute.

7. Ohno, Taiichi. 1988. *Toyota Production System: Beyond Large-Scale Production*, p. 122. New York, NY: Productivity Press.
8. Ibid.
9. Ohno, Taiichi. 2013. *Taiichi Ohno's Workplace Management: Special 100th Birthday Edition*, p. 103. New York, NY: McGraw-Hill.
10. Ohno, Taiichi. 1988. *Toyota Production System: Beyond Large-Scale Production*, p. 4. New York, NY: Productivity Press.
11. Ibid., p. 17.
12. Ibid., pp. 41–42.
13. Ohno, Taiichi. 2013. *Taiichi Ohno's Workplace Management: Special 100th Birthday Edition*, p. 64. New York, NY: McGraw-Hill.
14. Ohno, Taiichi. 1988. *Toyota Production System: Beyond Large-Scale Production*, p. 44. New York, NY: Productivity Press.
15. Ibid., p. 4.
16. Ibid., p.26.
17. Damodaran, Aswath. 2017. Margins by sector (US). New York University Stern School of Business. http://pages.stern.nyu.edu/~adamodar/New_Home_Page/datafile/margin.html.
18. Shimokawa, Koichi and Fujimoto, Takahiro. 2009. *The Birth of Lean*, p. 84. Cambridge, MA: The Lean Enterprise Institute.
19. Ohno, Taiichi. 1988. *Toyota Production System: Beyond Large-Scale Production*, p. 32. New York, NY: Productivity Press.
20. Ibid., p. 27.
21. Ibid., p. 29.
22. Shimokawa, Koichi and Fujimoto, Takahiro. 2009. *The Birth of Lean*, p. 75. Cambridge, MA: The Lean Enterprise Institute.
23. Ohno, Taiichi. 1988. *Toyota Production System: Beyond Large-Scale Production*, p. 33. New York, NY: Productivity Press.
24. Ibid., p. 29.
25. Shimokawa, Koichi and Fujimoto, Takahiro. 2009. *The Birth of Lean*, p. 83. Cambridge, MA: The Lean Enterprise Institute.
26. Monden, Yasuhiro. 2012. *Toyota Production System: An Integrated Approach to Just-in-Time*, 4th edn, p. 74. Boca Raton, FL: Productivity Press.
27. Ohno, Taiichi. 1988. *Toyota Production System: Beyond Large-Scale Production*, p. 27. New York, NY: Productivity Press.
28. Toyota Motor Manufacturing. Toyota production system terms. Georgetown, KY. Toyota. http://toyotaky.com/terms.asp.
29. Ohno, Taiichi. 1988. *Toyota Production System: Beyond Large-Scale Production*, p. 127. New York, NY: Productivity Press.
30. Ibid., p. 31.
31. Ibid., p. 96.

10

The Program: Jidoka, Quality at the Source

A program is an orderly set of procedures to attain a desired result.

> Unless such defective work is reduced, it is difficult to assure an adequate supply for the later process to withdraw ... Efforts to thoroughly stabilize and rationalize the processes are the key to successful implementation of automation. Only with this foundation can production leveling be effective.[1]

Jidoka came about because of an invention by Sakichi Toyota. Before automobiles, Toyota was well known for his spinning company, called Toyota Automatic Loom Works, later Toyota Boshuku, where he developed a loom that had a new feature. At this time, each loom was operated by an individual. The operator had to watch the machine constantly in case there was a problem with the thread breaking. One operator, one machine. Sakichi's invention stopped the loom when the thread broke or ran out. This prevented the loom from making defective cloth with broken thread. When the loom stopped, the operator would be required to correct the broken thread before continuing the operation. It was called "automation with a human element."[2] The meaning was that the machine recognized a problem, which was normally done by a human, and stopped. This prevented the machine from making poor-quality product.

This was a big development in the loom business. What it meant was an incredible increase in labor efficiency. Instead of one operator, one machine, an operator could now operate numerous machines, because they weren't required to stand over each one individually. This was breaking edge technology at the time. This same method was transferred to the automobile business later with the use of poka-yoke devices that sense abnormalities and help improve quality by preventing the production of poor-quality parts.

Furthermore, Toyota learned to separate machine work from human work. A simple example is that a machine is loaded with parts, a button is pushed to start the machine, and the operator moves on to the next machine. The human part is to load and start; the machine portion is to clamp, weld, and eject the part. This allows the operator to operate multiple machines.

Beyond "automation with a human touch," an additional method used to get quality at the source is to implement quality checks in each process. This information is part of the standard work for the operator. The operator is checking for something specific, or maybe several specific checks, on each part. The sources of these checks come from several places. Some checks are done because of the inability to make the check using a poka-yoke device. In this case, there is currently no way to automatically stop the process for a defect, so the operator makes the check. This could be visual or using some sort of checking device. These checks, likewise, prevent the production of poor-quality product.

Other checks are done due to feedback from a customer downstream. It's possible that the customer encounters a problem that is not being caught, or even known, by their supplier. The supplier checking for that failure mode would limit the chances of shipping a defect. Another source of a process quality check could be from issues arising from returned goods or warranty claims. In these instances, the defect has reached the outside customer, so these issues require urgent action.

For example, in Body, many nuts are welded onto parts using manual nut welders. Because of the nature of the machines, we were unable to install a poka-yoke device on manual nut welders. Parts sensors were in the next machine where this part was to be loaded. If a nut was left off, the machine would sense the missing nut and would not start. This required the attention of the operator to determine why. The missing nut would be discovered so that it could be attached before moving on to the next process. This is an important way Toyota prevents the passing on of poor quality to the next process.

I mentioned earlier (Chapter 7) that it was less important to implement standard work as one of the first steps in the Toyota Template, because you already had a way that things were being made. However, jidoka and visual quality checks can and should be implemented early on by adding quality checks to the current way. It's important that no poor quality is passed on, especially when operating in a pull system. The importance of quality in a pull system is emphasized by Ohno in the six kanban rules: "Rule 5 requires 100% defect-free products (that is, do not send anything defective to the subsequent process)."[3] Remember, there's no excess inventory to cover the problem now as there was in a push system. Additionally, it's a good idea to have 200% checks for defects as much as possible. In all cases, implementing quality checks in the process, at the source, is critical when implementing a pull system.

Program: Quality at the source.

Culture: Quality at the source is another important aspect in building the lean culture: placing checks in the process, explaining the need to the employees, and holding them accountable to properly follow the checks. This allows them to directly contribute to the quality of the end product by improving the quality of their individual daily work. The results are visible for all to see.

ENDNOTES

1. Ohno, Taiichi. 1988. *Toyota Production System: Beyond Large-Scale Production*, p. 41. New York, NY: Productivity Press.
2. Ohno, Taiichi. 2013. *Taiichi Ohno's Workplace Management: Special 100th Birthday Edition*, p. 61. New York, NY: McGraw-Hill.
3. Ohno, Taiichi. 1988. *Toyota Production System: Beyond Large-Scale Production*, p. 41. New York, NY: Productivity Press.

11

The Path: The Toyota Template

A path is an arrangement of actions to achieve something.

> The past is the past and what is important is the current condition and what we will do next to go beyond where we are today.[1]

The secret of the Toyota Production System (TPS) and the resulting culture is found in the actions, through trial and error, of Ohno and others over many years in implementation of the TPS. Remember, Ohno wasn't on a mission to create a system or a certain culture. He was on a mission to catch up with American auto manufacturers. The system and culture have been the result.

A lean culture has never resulted, and never will, from the haphazard application of tools. In tool-oriented lean initiatives, "having all the elements together as a system"[2] does not exist. Since not all the elements are present, they're not "practiced every day in a very consistent manner"[3] but instead, are implemented "in spurts."[4]

In the previous pages, the important concepts and methods that Taiichi Ohno implemented and the things that were emphasized to me during my time at Toyota have been laid out. Coincidentally, these elements are inclusive of the items in the original "Toyota House." Important additional concepts that are integral parts of the template and the culture have been added. For example, quick changeovers, accomplished with Single-Minute Exchange of Dies (SMED), are a crucial element that aids and enables the successful implementation of heijunka. And heijunka is a requirement for a just-in-time (JIT) production system. The result of the implementation of the "elements together as a system,"[5] the Toyota Template, is that the goal of the TPS, "the highest quality, at the lowest cost, in the shortest lead time," is continuously improved.

When the steps taken in building the most efficient and admired company in the world are understood, there exists a plan, the Toyota Template, that can be used as a guide in pursuit of efficiency. The template demonstrates an order of events that will result in the development of a lean culture along the way. This is how it happened at Toyota. That being said, this is not a cookie cutter approach to lean.

The TPS elements are solid and are not in dispute. The Toyota Template contains the important elements of the TPS to aid in a smoother transition away from traditional manufacturing. However, the template is in no way representative of the entire TPS.

WHEN SHOULD THE TEMPLATE BE IMPLEMENTED?

Here's what Ohno said about when …

> Kaizen should be done when times are good or when the company is profitable, since your efforts to streamline and make improvements when the company is poor are limited to reduction in staff. Even if you try to go lean and cut out the fat to improve business performance, when your business is in a very difficult position financially there is no fat to be cut. If you are cutting out muscle, which you need, then you cannot say that your efforts to become lean are succeeding. The most important thing about doing kaizen is to do kaizen when times are good, the economy is strong, and the company is profitable.[6]

The right time is when the company is profitable and when resources can be dedicated. There are no preconditions to becoming efficient.

IN WHAT ORDER SHOULD THE TEMPLATE BE IMPLEMENTED?

Ultimately, the goal is to arrive at a JIT system. The first consideration in the implementation order of the template is the current condition. This could influence the order of the elements. Some systems may already be in place and adequate. For example, a plant may have already minimized set-up times or have a well-functioning Total Productive Maintenance (TPM) program. The key is having as many of the concepts in place as possible prior to implementation of the pattern (flow, pull, and heijunka). This is because each of these concepts will greatly aid in the transition from a push to a pull method.

In terms of the order, context is important. Ohno developed most of these concepts and systems as he went along over many years, with the goal throughout to eliminate waste. As they say, hindsight is 20/20.

As I said, the gamechanger for Toyota was the implementation of the pattern of the template, consisting of continuous flow, pull, and heijunka. Continuous flow, which was done early, followed by pull many years later, and then heijunka were the keys that enabled Toyota to become a JIT manufacturer. Without these key elements, Toyota would not have realized the efficiency they enjoy today, because they would not have a JIT production system. For companies to become JIT producers, they must ultimately strive for the pattern.

Though the elements are intertwined and are all important, the Toyota Template arranges them in a logical implementation sequence, given what is now known. The sequence is determined, in part, by the sequence of events implemented by Taiichi Ohno and, in part, with the knowledge that the implementation of some elements before others makes sense. In addition to the sequence, some elements can be accomplished simultaneously. Implementing elements at the same time, if done properly, will accelerate the path toward JIT.

The two prerequisites necessary before moving forward with the Hoshin plan are

1. Will/skill
2. Plant first commitment.

    Leadership must be committed, and the skill set must be present. The focus is on the plant.

After the prerequisites are met, the Hoshin plan should be put in place.

3. *Hoshin Kanri*: Develop a plan for implementation based on the template and the current condition.
4. Waste elimination, problem-solving, jidoka, SMED, TPM/machine back-up, 5S.

    These elements can be accomplished simultaneously. They involve some classroom learning but mostly are taught, learned, and practiced at the worksite. Each should be driven using 8-Step problem-solving with an accompanying A3 that is reviewed regularly. Each of these will involve hands-on implementation over an extended period. Keep at it until they're routinized in daily work. Many results of the implementation will be reflected in Key Performance Indicators going forward.

5. Continuous flow

   This element is important for reasons cited in Chapter 9. Continuous flow may already partially exist in the current condition. One-piece flow production areas are the most important to consider. There are many advantages to continuous flow in these areas, and this should be the goal. There's one-time cost associated with rearranging the floor, and there's potentially daily cost associated with a decision not to rearrange.

6. Pull

   Pull involves two major components:

   a. *Batch build processes*: The next step toward a JIT system in the plant is to install a pull system in batch build processes. The reduction in changeover times, done previously, was in preparation to implement the linkage between batch building and one-piece flow. This is accomplished with the Triangle Kanban. The kanban will eliminate schedules. Pulling in batch build processes is a significant change. Visually, it's much easier to manage for supervision and easier for employees to understand. This is because the kanban institutes a standard production method that schedules production based on actual use and a build order based on first-in, first-out (FIFO). Implementing the Triangle should be carefully planned, coordinated, and monitored because of the change from schedules (push) to kanban (pull). This is done before pulling in the one-piece flow processes, because it will decrease shortages when one-piece flow is implemented.

   b. *One-piece flow processes*: Establish a sequence for orders/jobs to be pulled through the plant. If there are reliable data suggesting a way to level load now, try it. Pull orders through the plant in the sequence. This establishes a pace for production. As this is done, bottleneck, staffing, machine, and material issues will become visible. It's likely that many previous problems will no longer exist. The focus changes from schedule attainment to buffers, and the sense of urgency will increase. At this point, problems will pop up that have always existed but weren't visible or urgent before. With good problem-solving skills, some of these issues can be anticipated and planned for as part of the A3.

7. *Standard work*: As stated earlier (Chapter 7), standard work is implemented after, or during, the implementation of the pull system.

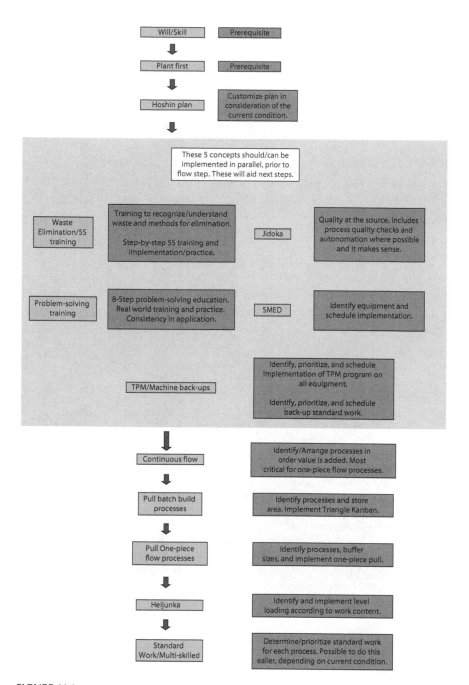

FIGURE 11.1
The Toyota Template Flow Chart.

This is because there already exists a certain way that products were made in the prior push system. In a pull system, the standard work changes, because a pace based on TAKT time is established. Though the work content to make a particular item may not change, where the steps are done could change. If time is spent writing standard work prior to pull, much of it will likely need to be rewritten.

The flow chart in Figure 11.1 illustrates this sequence.

As stated at the beginning of the chapter, the intention of the Toyota Template is to understand the critically important elements of the TPS, analyze the sequence of implementation as the system developed, and put these elements in a logical order of implementation based on current knowledge. It will guide any organization to focus on "the current condition and what [they] will do next to go beyond where [they] are today"[7] to achieve greater productivity and a problem-solving culture. It has worked well for Toyota in many diverse cultures over many years, and it will work for you.

ENDNOTES

1. Ohno, Taiichi. 2013. *Taiichi Ohno's Workplace Management: Special 100th Birthday Edition*, p. xi. New York, NY: McGraw-Hill.
2. Liker, Jeffrey K. 2004. *The Toyota Way, 14 Management Principles From The World's Greatest Manufacturer*, p. 27. New York, NY: McGraw-Hill.
3. Liker, Jeffrey K. 2004. *The Toyota Way, 14 Management Principles From The World's Greatest Manufacturer*, p. 27. New York, NY: McGraw-Hill.
4. Liker, Jeffrey K. 2004. *The Toyota Way, 14 Management Principles From The World's Greatest Manufacturer*, p. 27. New York, NY: McGraw-Hill.
5. Liker, Jeffrey K. 2004. *The Toyota Way, 14 Management Principles From The World's Greatest Manufacturer*, p. 27. New York, NY: McGraw-Hill.
6. Ohno, Taiichi. 2013. *Taiichi Ohno's Workplace Management: Special 100th Birthday Edition*, p. 52. New York, NY: McGraw-Hill.
7. Ohno, Taiichi. 2013. *Taiichi Ohno's Workplace Management: Special 100th Birthday Edition*, p. xi. New York, NY: McGraw-Hill.

12

The Proof: TPS Results

Proof is the evidence that something is true.

The Toyota Template, with its focus on production, is in no way meant to exclude other parts of the Toyota Production System (TPS), particularly the many benefits enjoyed by their employees and the communities where they live. I would be remiss if I didn't mention a few that are sometimes taken for granted. For example, the many Human Resources policies that demonstrate fairness and respect for their team members. Or their multi-tiered hiring process that seeks out those who match their desired mental, emotional, and personal attributes. I also did not delve into the highest environmental standards met by Toyota, which demonstrate their commitment to the well-being of the local community and the world. Or their generosity in gifts to numerous local endeavors. There was no mention of the many visible, tangible benefits provided to team members, such as onsite 24-hour daycare, an onsite pharmacy, an on-site fitness center, a team store, and a credit union at the Georgetown facility.

Toyota has shown their commitment to their employees and the community in other ways, too. When the Toyota plant was completed in 1988, the population of Georgetown, Kentucky was around 11,000 people. With the addition of an employer of this size, Toyota realized the town would grow quite a bit, with many employees locating there with their families. Today, the population is over 30,000. In anticipation of what was about to happen, Toyota made a commitment to the Scott County School System.

On January 20, 1988, Toyota Motor Manufacturing, Kentucky (TMMK), Inc. and the Scott County Board of Education signed an agreement confirming that TMMK would pay the school system annual in-lieu-of tax payments over the next 20 years. A portion of the construction financing for the manufacturing facility was done through Industrial Revenue

Bonds, making the financed property exempt from property taxes for the life of the Bonds. Each year, TMMK pays the school what TMMK would pay in property taxes.

Payments to the school system over the 20-year period amounted to $28,865,045.[1]

Take a look at some of the results Toyota has gleaned relative to the competition from their incredible business system. It's astonishing how well they perform in so many areas.

In the *Forbes* ranking of the 100 most valuable brands in the world for 2017, Toyota ranked #8. They were the only car maker in the top 15 (Figure 12.1).

The Detroit News analyzed earnings/vehicle sold in 2014. Though many factors contribute to earnings, it's interesting that Toyota's earnings are more than the combined earnings of Ford, FCA, and GM for 2014 (Figure 12.2).

Cars.com ranked most American-made cars for 2016. The ranking considers such factors as whether the car was bought and built in the United States. and the percentage of domestic parts used. Cars with a domestic content less than 75% or built outside of the United States are not listed (Figure 12.3).

Out of only eight cars that qualified for the list, Toyota occupies two of the top three places, including the #1 slot. Interestingly, foreign nameplates hold the top five places (Figure 12.3).

Rank	Brand value	2017 ($B)
1	*Toyota*	*41.1*
2	Mercedes-Benz	29.2
3	BMW	28.7
4	Honda	24
5	Audi	14.1
6	Ford	13.8
7	Chevrolet	10.3
8	Porsche	9.6
9	Lexus	9.1
10	Nissan	9

FIGURE 12.1
Car brand values (2017). (Adapted from Forbes. 2017. The world's most valuable brands. 2017 ranking. www.forbes.com/powerful-brands/list/2/#tab:rank.).

Toyota	$2,726
Ford	$994
FCA	$850
GM	$654

FIGURE 12.2

Average earnings/vehicle sold (2014). (Adapted from Wayland, Michael. 2015. Toyota's per-car profits lap Detroit's Big 3 automakers. February 22. http://www.detroitnews.com/story/business/autos/2015/02/22/toyota-per-car-profits-beat-ford-gm-chrysler/23852189/.)

1. *Toyota Camry (made in Georgetown, KY)*
2. Honda Accord
3. *Toyota Sienna (made in Princeton, IN)*
4. Honda Odyssey
5. Honda Pilot
6. Chevrolet Traverse
7. GMC Acadia
8. Buick Enclave

FIGURE 12.3

American-made index (2016). (Adapted from Mays, Kelsey. 2016. The 2016 Cars.com American-Made Index. June 28. https://www.cars.com/articles/the-2016-carscom-american-made-index-1420684865874/.).

Edmunds.com put together a list of the projected retained value of cars after 5 years on the road. The #1 vehicle in each category is shown along with the projected retained value for each. Of the 24 categories, Toyota/Lexus brands lead in 8 (33%) (Figure 12.4).

Since Toyota began manufacturing cars in North America, they've made steady gains in market share, more than doubling their market share since 1985 (Figure 12.5).

Toyota is the clear leader in the hybrid car market according to Wardsauto.com (Figure 12.6).

ENVIRONMENT

The U.S. Environmental Protection Agency (EPA) has certified 70 manufacturing plants for their "superior energy performance" *five of these were Toyota plants.*[2] The plants receiving the Energy Star designation are in Kentucky (2), Indiana, Mississippi, and Texas.[3]

Category	Model	Retained value %
Midsize Traditional SUV	Jeep Wrangler	62.7
Midsize Truck	*Toyota Tacoma*	*66.0*
Heavy Duty Truck	Ram 2500	58.6
Large Truck	*Toyota Tundra*	*58.6*
Large Traditional SUV	GMC Yukon	52.6
Midrange Sports Car	Chevrolet Corvette	53.9
Compact Crossover SUV	Honda CR-V	54.9
Midsize Crossover SUV	*Toyota Highlander*	*56.9*
Entry Sports Car	Ford Mustang	54.2
Compact Car	Subaru WRX	58.3
Subcompact Car	Honda Fit	53.8
Large Commercial Van	Mercedes-Benz Sprinter	52.6
Entry Luxury SUV	*Lexus NX 200t*	*49.1*
Small Commercial Van	Mercedes-Benz Metris	48.5
Minivan	Honda Odyssey	48.5
Midrange Luxury SUV	*Lexus GX 460*	*50.9*
Premium Luxury SUV	Mercedes-Benz G-Class	55.9
Premium Sports Car	Porsche 911	51.5
Large Crossover SUV	GMC Acadia	45.6
Entry Luxury Car	*Lexus IS 350*	*50.6*
Midsize Car	*Toyota Camry*	*48.1*
Large Car	*Toyota Avalon*	*47.2*
Midrange Luxury Car	BMW M3	50.1
Premium Luxury Car	Porsche Panamera	47.9

FIGURE 12.4

Projected 5-year retained value of 2016 Vehicles. (Adapted from edmunds. 2016. Edmunds.com recognizes top new car models and brands with 2016 Best Retained Value® Awards. April. https://www.edmunds.com/about/press/edmundscom-recognizes-top-new-car-models-and-brands-with-2016-best-retained-value-awards.html.).

	1985	1995	2014	2016
GM	40.4	32.2	17.4	17.0
Ford	21.3	25.5	14.7	14.6
Toyota	*6*	*7.2*	*14.1*	*13.9*
Chrysler	11.8	14.3	12.5	12.6

FIGURE 12.5

U.S. market share (%). (Adapted from www.epi.org/publication/the-decline-and-resurgence-of-the-u-s-auto-industry/U.S. Vehicle Sales Market Share by Company, 1961–2016 Feb 6, 2017.)

Manufacturer	2016
Toyota/Lexus	*65%*
Ford	12%
Hyundai	5%
Honda	3%
Chevrolet	1%

FIGURE 12.6

U.S. hybrid sales (2016). (Adapted from www.wardsauto.com/engines/toyota-leads-hybrid-market-record-sales-2016. Toyota Leads Hybrid Market to Record Sales in 2016 Mar 1, 2017.)

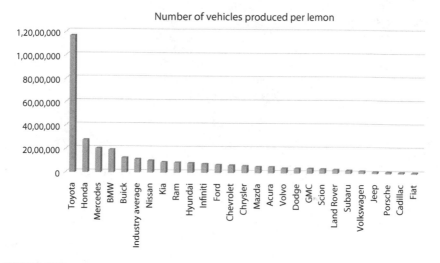

FIGURE 12.7

Autoguide.com Lemon List (2015). (Adapted from AutoGuide.com staff. 2016. Toyota tops, Fiat flops in AutoGuide's 1st annual lemon list. January 28. AutoGuide. http://www.autoguide.com/auto-news/2016/01/toyota-tops-fiat-flops-in-autoguide-s-1st-annual-lemon-list.html.)

Autoguide.com put out an interesting "Lemon List" of cars made in 2010 or later that included only complaints made in the calendar year 2015. They normalized the data for an apples-to-apples comparison between brands. Toyota averaged 1 reported lemon per 11,655,566 cars. Second on the list was Honda, which averaged 1 lemon per 2,782,495 cars. Toyota produced a lemon at one-quarter the rate of #2 Honda. The industry average was 1 per 1,144,744.

However, Toyota are so much better than everyone else that they skew the average. If Toyota's data are taken out of the survey, the industry average is 1 per 740,512 cars. The industry average goes up more than 30% without Toyota (Figure 12.7).

The Department of Energy's Better Buildings, Better Plant program is focused on industrial energy efficiency. The goal is to reduce energy intensity by 25% over 10 years. Toyota's cumulative improvement was 27% in 2012 after 4 years.

ENDNOTES

1. The Official Website of Toyota Motor Manufacturing, Kentucky, Inc. Terms. http://toyotaky.com/comm3.asp.
2. Adapted from www.forbes.com/powerful-brands/list/2/#tab:rank.
3. McDonald, Jason. 2016. EPA announces Toyota Motor Manufacturing achieved 2015 ENERGY STAR Certification. February 24. U.S. Environmental Protection Agency. https://19january2017snapshot.epa.gov/newsreleases/epa-announces-toyota-motor-manufacturing-achieved-2015-energy-star-certification_.html

13

The Perceptions: Mental Images

Perceptions are feelings or impressions of something.

Previously, I addressed the problem with the general tool orientation that's been so common in lean efforts and that these tool efforts aren't consistent with the statement that "Many good companies have respect for individuals, and practice kaizen and other TPS tools ... But what is important is having all the elements together as a system. It must be practiced every day in a very consistent manner, not in spurts."[1] The tools individually aren't a system that is consistently practiced. Since this is "the key"[2] and having experienced "all the elements together in a system,"[3] I agree.

This tool approach has led to another failure mode. Many times, an area in the plant is selected to "lean out," the idea being that after the tools and concepts are applied in one area, they can then be transferred to other areas. I can see where this viewpoint might make sense and, in fact, could possibly work. The problem with this approach is that it purposely ignores many important conditions. For example, attempting to lean out one area when in a push system is fraught with problems. Pulling in one area of a plant while everyone else is pushing is very difficult to sustain. The synchronization problem makes this difficult. This could work if the entire value stream for the chosen area is addressed, from beginning to end, but this is a difficult strategy to work out.

Another common position advocated is that a lean implementation needs to choose places where it's possible to obtain "quick wins" to prove that lean works and obtain buy-in. It seems that success depends on convincing employees that it works. Explaining to employees why things are done is important and should always be done, but not with a "quick win" strategy. There's no such thing as a quick win when implementing the Toyota Template.

As has been proved at Toyota numerous times, the template works. If there's any doubt, visit the Georgetown, Kentucky facility; the Blue Springs, Mississippi facility; or any of the other Toyota facilities. There's no need to prove anything. Besides, a company should already be 100% committed, have a good implementation plan, and have communicated both of these to the employees prior to doing anything on the floor. If employees must be convinced with quick wins, there's a lack of management commitment.

Finally, there's the strategy to choose an area to improve based on some pie-in-the-sky dollar savings. For the same reasons as trying to lean out an area, this is not good. Both strategies emphasize a "place" based on dollars instead of a "problem" based on the current condition. The template is about implementing the right processes that produce the right results. Reduced costs will be one of the many right results. In the beginning, choosing projects based on some cost savings is indicative of a tool approach. The elements work when they are together as part of a system and implemented with a practical, common-sense strategy based on the current condition in the environment.

ENDNOTES

1. Liker, Jeffrey K. 2004. *The Toyota Way: 14 Management Principles from the World's Greatest Manufacturer.* p. 27. New York, NY: McGraw-Hill.
2. Ibid.
3. Ibid.

14

The Post Script: Personal Matters

A post script is a footnote at the end.

I was fortunate to be exposed to the Toyota Production System as a young man. I'd never been in an automobile plant, and I had no idea what I was about to see and learn. This was an "eyes wide open" experience for me. And it came on like a whirlwind. Only 12 days after starting at Toyota, barely out of orientation and not knowing anyone very well, I was off to Japan for a month of training. I was part of the seventh group to go over to our mother plant, Tsutsumi, and I went with 49 other newly hired team-mates, 6 of whom were also from Body Weld. My team member # was 531. When we left, Body Weld was technically still a construction site. When we returned, it had been turned over to production.

I have so many great memories of the trip. We were treated to a nice greeting ceremony where I experienced sushi for the first time. I distinctly recall asking what the meat was on the stick in front of me and being told it was "sparrow." One weekend, a few of our group took the bullet train from Nagoya to Kyoto in the interior mountains of Japan. The snow-capped mountains in February were beautiful. The Buddhist temples in Kyoto are some of the largest wooden buildings in the world. Interesting place. I remember seeing the employee parking lot at the plant and wondering how my trainer would find his car. It seemed that 75% of the cars were white. In a nutshell, it was explained to me that the Japanese, being one race, had similar tastes. And that if someone owned a red car, its resale value would suffer. Not sure about that part? Interesting nonetheless.

Far and away the most lasting memory of the trip is the time I spent with my personal trainer. He was old enough to be my father and had spent his entire working career with Toyota. He was kind and friendly, gracious, neat, organized, professional, and most of all a patient teacher. He was the Group

Leader of the group where I trained. He always carried a Japanese/English translation dictionary with him, as he could speak little English and I spoke no Japanese. In between training, we'd sit in the break room and slowly try to become better acquainted. He invited me over for dinner one Saturday, where I met his lovely wife. She'd cooked a great Japanese meal and provided a fork, spoon, and knife for me, even though they didn't use them. We sat on the floor around a round table under a warm blanket and ate, talked, and laughed. On another night, he took me to a steakhouse after work. I think he wanted to make me feel a bit more at home. That's just how he was.

A few months after I returned home, my trainer came to the plant in Georgetown for 3 months to set up some of the systems and to further our training. By this time, there were six or seven members in our group. He fit right in and made a strong impression on everyone. I returned the favor and invited him over for dinner and took him sightseeing. I felt grateful and indebted for his friendship and example. When the time came for him to return to Japan, we were sad to say goodbye. He wrote a four-page, handwritten letter in English and read it to the group. In it, he mentioned every member by name and had something kind to say about each person. His last words for us at his departure are shown in Figure 14.1.

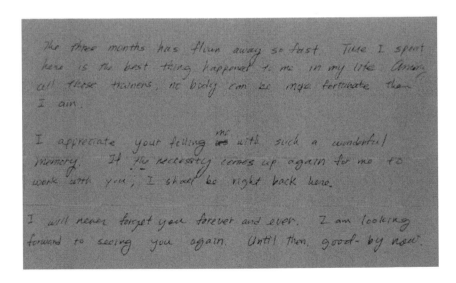

FIGURE 14.1
Part of the farewell letter written to the work group upon his departure by my personal trainer, Mr. Itaru Baba (1988).

Index

Autoguide.com, 91
Auxiliary work, 29

Batch build processes, 61, 64, 74–75, 84
Baton passing zone, 58
Better Plant program, 92
Blue sky project. *see* Global Body Line
    (GBL)
Body Weld Dept, 46, 54, 95
Boshuku, Toyota, 77
Buffers, 63–64, 71–72

Cars.com, 88
Catchball, 22
Combination banner, 10
Continuous flow, 84
    description, 58–59
    overview, 57–58
Countermeasures, 52–53

Days Inventory Outstanding (DIO), 24
Defects, and waste elimination, 31
The Detroit News, 88
DIO. *see* Days Inventory Outstanding
    (DIO)
Downstream process, 62

Earnings before interest, taxes,
    depreciation and amortization
    (EBITDA), 65
EBITDA. *see* Earnings before interest,
    taxes, depreciation and
    amortization (EBITDA)
Edmunds.com, 89
Energy Star, 89
Environmental Protection Agency (EPA),
    89
EPA. *see* Environmental Protection
    Agency (EPA)
Excess inventory, 30–31

FBL. *see* Flexible Body Line (FBL)

FIFO. *see* First-in, first-out (FIFO)
First-in, first-out (FIFO), 69
5S (Seiri, Seiton, Seiso, Seiketsu, and
    Shitsuke) program, 31–34, 83
Flexible Body Line (FBL), 17
Follow-up, 53
Forbes, 88

GBL. *see* Global Body Line (GBL)
General Motors (GM), 1–2
Global Body Line (GBL), 17
GM. *see* General Motors (GM)

Heijunka, 10–11, 68–72
Honda, 91
Hoshin Kanri plan, 21–25, 83
    KPI rules, 23–24
    measuring overall progress, 24–25
    overview, 21–23

Industrial Revenue Bonds, 87–88

JI. *see* Job Instruction (JI)
Jidoka, 77–79
JIT. *see* Just-in-time (JIT) systems
JM. *see* Job Methods (JM)
Job Instruction (JI), 40
Job Methods (JM), 40
Job Relations (JR), 40
JR. *see* Job Relations (JR)
Just-in-time (JIT) systems, 9, 38, 84
    description, 60–67
    overview, 57–58

Kaizen events, 6, 9, 50–51
Kaizen Train-the-Trainer, 49
Kanban, 10, 18, 67–68
Key Performance Indicators (KPIs), 16
    and Hoshin Kanri plan, 23–24
Key Productivity Indicators (KPIs). *see*
    Key Performance Indicators
    (KPIs)

KPIs. *see* Key Performance Indicators (KPIs)

Lean transformations, 5
"Lemon List," 91
Little's Law, 66

Material and Information Flow Diagram (MIFD), 6
Material Resource Planning (MRP), 61
MIFD. *see* Material and Information Flow Diagram (MIFD)
MRP. *see* Material Resource Planning (MRP)
Multi-skilled employee, 39–42

NUMMI, 1

Ohno, Taiichi, 3, 13, 18, 27–28, 35, 39, 46, 52–53, 57–59, 65–66, 79, 81–83
    7 WASTES of (*see* Waste elimination)
One-piece flow processes, 84
On-time-delivery (OTD), 24, 49
OTD. *see* On-time-delivery (OTD)
Over-processing, and waste elimination, 30
Overproduction, 28–29

Parts withdrawal kanban, 67–68
Patois problem-solving language, 45–56
Plant first principle, 13–14, 83
"Point kaizen" emphasis, 70
Predicaments, 5–11
Production instruction/signal kanban, 68
Production leveling, 72
Pull systems. *see* Just-in-time (JIT) systems
Push systems, 7–8
    description, 60–67
    overview, 57–58

QC. *see* Quality Circle (QC)
Quality at source, 77–79
Quality Circle (QC), 55

Scott County Board of Education, 87
Scott County School System, 87

Seiri, Seiton, Seiso, Seiketsu, and Shitsuke (5S) program, 31–34
Selectivity bank, 72
Set-up time reduction, 72–75
Signal kanban/production instruction, 68
Single-Minute Exchange of Dies (SMED) method, 9, 72–75
S.M.A.R.T. *see* Specific, Measurable, Achievable, Realistic, and Time-targeted (S.M.A.R.T.)
SMED. *see* Single-Minute Exchange of Dies (SMED) method
Specific, Measurable, Achievable, Realistic, and Time-targeted (S.M.A.R.T.), 22, 51
Standard work practice, 84, 86
    multi-skilled employee, 39–42
    overview, 35–37
    teamwork, 39–42
    Total Productive Maintenance (TPM), 37–39
Straight line thinking, 27
Supermarket strategy, 61

TAKT time, 39, 42, 63, 66, 75, 86
Teamwork, 39–42
Therefore test, 52
Timing problem, 68
TMMK. *see* Toyota Motor Manufacturing, Kentucky (TMMK)
Total Productive Maintenance (TPM), 37–39, 82
Toyota, Eiji, 3
Toyota, Kiichiro, 3, 58
Toyota, Sakichi, 77
Toyota Automatic Loom Works, 77
Toyota House, 81
Toyota Motor Manufacturing, Kentucky (TMMK), 17, 87
Toyota Production System (TPS)
    Hoshin Kanri plan, 21–25
        KPI rules, 23–24
        measuring overall progress, 24–25
        overview, 21–23
    overview, 1–3
    plant first principle, 13–14
    predicaments, 5–11
    standard work practice

multi-skilled employee, 39–42
overview, 35–37
patois problem-solving language,
45–56
teamwork, 39–42
Total Productive Maintenance
(TPM), 37–39
waste elimination
defects, 31
excess inventory, 30–31
5S program, 31–34
over-processing, 30
overproduction, 28–29
overview, 27–28
transportation, 29–30
unnecessary motion, 31
waiting, 29
will/skill, 15–19
Toyota Template, 81–86
The Toyota Way (Liker), 18
TPM. *see* Total Productive Maintenance
(TPM)
TPS. *see* Toyota Production System (TPS)
Training Within Industry (TWI), 40
Transportation, and waste, 29–30
Triangle kanban system, 10, 18, 73–74, 84

TWI. *see* Training Within
Industry (TWI)

Unnecessary motion, 31
Upstream process, 62

Value Stream Map (VSM), 6
Visual quality checks, 78

Wardsauto.com, 89
Waste elimination
defects, 31
excess inventory, 30–31
5S program, 31–34
over-processing, 30
overproduction, 28–29
overview, 27–28
transportation, 29–30
unnecessary motion, 31
waiting, 29
5-Why exercise, 51–52
Will/skill, 15–19
WIP. *see* Work in process (WIP)
Work-in-process (WIP), 6, 59

X-Matrix, 23